HABITS
OF A
HAPPY BRAIN

HABITS
OF A
HAPPY
BRAIN

Retrain Your Brain to Boost Your Serotonin, Dopamine, Oxytocin, & Endorphin Levels

LORETTA GRAZIANO BREUNING, PHD

Adams Media

New York   London   Toronto   Sydney   New Delhi

Adams Media
An Imprint of Simon & Schuster, Inc.
57 Littlefield Street
Avon, Massachusetts 02322

For information about special discounts for bulk purchases, please contact Simon & Schuster Special Sales at 1-866-506-1949 or business@simonandschuster.com.

The Simon & Schuster Speakers Bureau can bring authors to your live event. For more information or to book an event contact the Simon & Schuster Speakers Bureau at 1-866-248-3049 or visit our website at www.simonspeakers.com.

Manufactured in the United States of America

20 19 18 17 16 15 14 13 12

Library of Congress Cataloging-in-Publication Data has been applied for.

ISBN 978-1-4405-9050-4
ISBN 978-1-4405-9051-1 (ebook)

for David Attenborough, who told the truth
about the conflict in nature
and
for my wonderful husband, Bill

CONTENTS

INTRODUCTION

When you feel good, your brain is releasing dopamine, serotonin, oxytocin, or endorphin. You want more of these great feelings because your brain is designed to seek them. But you don't always get it, and that's natural too. Our brain doesn't release a happy chemical until it sees a way to meet a survival need, like food, safety, and social support. And then, you only get a quick spurt before your brain returns to neutral so it's ready for the next "survival opportunity." This is why you feel up and down. It's nature's operating system!

Many people have habits that are bad for survival. How does that happen if our brain rewards behaviors that are good for survival? When a happy-chemical spurt is over, you feel like something is wrong. You look for a reliable way to feel good again, fast. Anything that worked before built a pathway in your brain. We all have such happy habits: from snacking to exercising, whether it's spending or saving, partying or solitude, arguing or making up. But none of these habits can make you happy all the time because your brain doesn't work that way. Every happy-chemical spurt is quickly metabolized and you have to do more to get more. You can end up overdoing a happy habit to the point of unhappiness.

Wouldn't it be great if you could turn on your happy chemicals in new ways? Wouldn't it be nice to feel good while doing things that are actually good for you? You can, when you understand your mammal brain. Then you'll know what turns on the happy chemicals in nature, and how your brain can substitute new habits for old ones. You can design a new happy habit and wire it into your neurons. This book helps you do that in forty-five days.

You don't need much time or money to build a new neural pathway; you need courage and focus, because you must repeat a new behavior for forty-five days whether or not it feels good.

Why doesn't it feel good to start a new habit? Your old habits are like well-paved highways in your brain. New behaviors are hard to activate because they're just narrow trails in your jungle of neurons. Unknown trails feel dangerous and exhausting, so we're tempted to stick to our familiar highways instead. But with courage and commitment, you will build a new highway, and on Day Forty-Six, it will feel so good that you will build another.

Warning: This book is about *your* brain, not about other people's brains. If you are in the habit of blaming your neurochemical ups and downs on others, you will not find support here. But you needn't blame yourself, either—you can make peace with your mammalian neurochemistry instead of finding fault with it. This book shows you how.

We'll explore the brain chemicals that make us happy and unhappy. We'll see how they work in animals, and why they have a job to do. Then we'll see how the brain creates habits, and why bad ones are so difficult to break. Finally, we'll embark on a forty-five-day plan that explains how to choose a new behavior and how to find the courage and focus you need to repeat it without fail. This edition of the book contains a lot of new exercises and interactive features that help you take each step. You will like the results—a happier, healthier you!

1 | YOUR INNER MAMMAL

Our Survival-Focused Brain

Your brain is inherited from people who survived. This may seem obvious, but when you look closer at the huge survival challenges of the past, it seems like a miracle that all of *your* direct ancestors kept their genes alive. You have inherited a brain that is focused on survival. You may not think you are focused on survival, but when you worry about being late for a meeting or eating the wrong food, your survival brain is at work. When you worry about being invited to a party or having a bad hair day, your survival brain sees the risk of social exclusion, which was a very real threat to your ancestors. Once you're safe from immediate threats like hunger, cold, and predators, your brain scans for other potential threats. It's not easy being a survivor!

Consciously, you know that bad hair is not a survival threat, but brains tuned to social opportunities made more copies of themselves. Natural selection built a brain that rewards you with a good feeling when you see an opportunity for your genes and alarms you with a bad feeling when you lose an opportunity. No conscious intent to spread your genes is necessary for a small social setback to trigger your natural alarm system.

These responses are rooted in your brain's desire to survive, but they're not hard-wired. We are not born to seek specific foods or avoid specific predators the way animals often are. We are born to wire ourselves from life experience. We start building that wiring from the moment of birth. Anything that made you feel good built pathways to your happy chemicals that tell you "this is good for me." Whatever felt bad built pathways that say "this is bad for me." By the time you were seven years old, your core circuits were built. Seven may seem young, since a seven-year-old has little insight into its long-term survival needs. But seven years is a long time for a creature in nature to be practically defenseless. This is why we end up with core neurochemical circuits that don't always match up with our survival needs.

In short, your brain has some quirks:

1. It cares for the survival of your genes as urgently as it cares for your body.
2. It wires itself from early experience, though that's an imperfect guide to adult survival.

This is why our neurochemical ups and downs can be so hard to make sense of.

How Do Chemicals Make Us Happy?

The feeling we call "happiness" comes from four special brain chemicals: *dopamine*, *endorphin*, *oxytocin*, and *serotonin*. These "happy chemicals" turn on when your brain sees something good for your survival. Then they turn off, so they're ready to activate again when something good crosses your path.

Each happy chemical triggers a different good feeling:

- **Dopamine** produces the joy of finding things that meet your needs—the "Eureka! I got it!" feeling.
- **Endorphin** produces oblivion that masks pain—often called euphoria.
- **Oxytocin** produces the feeling of being safe with others—now called bonding.
- **Serotonin** produces the feeling of being respected by others—pride.

"I don't define happiness in those terms," you may say. That's because neurochemicals work without words. But you can easily see how strong these motivations are in others. And research illuminates these impulses in animals. As for yourself, your verbal inner voice may seem like your whole thought process until you know the chemistry of your inner mammal.

FOUR HAPPY CHEMICALS

Dopamine: the joy of finding what you seek

Endorphin: the oblivion that masks pain

Oxytocin: the comfort of social alliances

Serotonin: the security of social importance

How Do Happy Chemicals Work?

Happy chemicals are controlled by tiny brain structures that all mammals have in common: the hippocampus, amygdala, pituitary, hypothalamus, and other parts collectively known as the limbic system. The human limbic system is surrounded by a huge cortex. Your limbic system and cortex are always working together to keep you alive and keep your DNA alive. Each has its special job:

- Your **cortex** looks for patterns in the present that match patterns you connected in the past.
- Your **limbic system** releases neurochemicals that tell your body "this is good for you, go toward it," and "this is bad for you, avoid it." Your body doesn't always act on these messages because your cortex can override them. If the cortex overrides a message, it generates an alternative and your limbic system reacts to it. So your cortex can inhibit your limbic system momentarily, but your mammal brain is the core of who you

are. Your cortex directs attention and sifts information, but your limbic brain sparks the action.

Each Chemical Has a Job

Your inner mammal rewards you with good feelings when you do something good for your survival. Each of the happy chemicals motivates a different type of survival behavior:

- **Dopamine** motivates you to get what you need, even when it takes a lot of effort.
- **Endorphin** motivates you to ignore pain, so you can escape from harm when you're injured.
- **Oxytocin** motivates you to trust others, to find safety in companionship.
- **Serotonin** motivates you to get respect, which expands your mating opportunities and protects your offspring.

You might come up with different motivations in your verbal brain, but your inner mammal decides what feels good.

> **HAPPY SURVIVAL MOTIVES**
> Dopamine: seek rewards
> Endorphin: ignore physical pain
> Oxytocin: build social alliances
> Serotonin: get respect from others

The mammal brain motivates a body to go toward things that trigger happy chemicals and avoid things that trigger unhappy chemicals. You can restrain yourself from acting on a neurochemical impulse, but then your brain generates another impulse, seeking the next-best way to meet your survival needs. You're not a slave to your animal impulses, but nor do you just operate on pure data, even if you believe you are doing that. You are always looking for a way to feel good, deciding whether to act on it, and then looking for the next best way of feeling good.

Good Feelings Help Animals Meet Needs

Animals accept their neurochemical impulses without expecting a verbal rationale. That's why animals can help us make sense of our own brain chemicals. The goal here is not to glorify animals or primitive impulses; it is to know what turns on our happy chemicals.

For example, a hungry lion is happy when she sees prey she can reach. This is not philosophical happiness, but a physical state of arousal that releases energy for the hunt. Lions often fail in their hunts, so they choose their targets carefully to avoid running out of energy and starving to death. When a lion sees a gazelle she knows she can get, she's thrilled. Her dopamine surges, which revs up her motor to pounce.

A thirsty elephant is happy when he finds water. The good feeling of quenching his thirst triggers dopamine, which makes permanent connections in his neurons. That helps him find water again in the future. He need not "try" to learn where water is. Dopamine simply paves a neural pathway. The next time he sees any sign of a water hole, electricity zips down the path to his happy chemicals. The good feeling tells him "here is what you need." When he's exhausted and dehydrated, a sign of a reward at hand triggers the good feeling that spurs him on. Without effort or intent, happy chemicals promote survival.

But happy chemicals don't flow constantly. The lion only gets more happy chemicals when she finds more prey, and the elephant only releases them when he sees a way to meet a need.

There is no free happy chemical in the state of nature. Good feelings evolved because they get us to do things that promote survival.

Comparing the Limbic Systems and Cortexes of a Variety of Animals

Animals make survival decisions with very little cortex. Their limbic system is enough to decide what's good for them. It motivates them to approach when a good feeling is released and to avoid when a bad feeling is released. This simple system kept our animal ancestors alive for millions of years and is still working inside us.

The following figure shows how the basic chassis of our brain stayed the same while the size of the parts changed immensely. Nature tends to build on what's there instead of starting over with a blank sheet. Mammals built onto the reptile brain and humans built onto the mammal brain. We humans have a large stock of extra neurons ready to wire in new experience. Reptiles have a miniscule stock of neurons so they rarely adapt to new experience. But the reptile brain is skilled at scanning the world for threats and opportunities. If you ever feel like you are of two minds, or that your mind is going in different directions, this chart makes it easy to see why.

Comparing brain parts

cortex	extra neurons that store life experience by growing and interconnecting
limbic system	structures that manage neuro-chemicals, such as the amygdala, hippocampus, hypothalamus
reptilian brain	the cerebellum and brain stem (medulla oblongata and pons), which manage routine bodily functions
human	
chimpanzee	
gazelle	
mouse	
lizard	

How the Human Limbic System and Cortex Work Together

Your big cortex makes you different from other animals. You can keep building new neural pathways and thus keep fine-tuning your efforts to meet your needs. But man does not live by cortex alone. You need your limbic system to know what's good for you. Your cortex sees the world as a chaos of raw detail until your limbic system creates the feeling that something is good or bad for you. You may have gotten the idea that your limbic brain is the bad guy and your cortex is the good guy, but it's more helpful to know how they need each other. Your limbic system needs your cortex to make sense of your pleasure and pain. But your cortex cannot produce happy chemicals. If you want to be happy, you have to get it from your limbic system.

The limbic system cannot process language. When you talk to yourself, it's all in your cortex. That's why the limbic system never tells you in words why it activates a happy or unhappy chemical. So you might think, "I'm not feeling that way" just because you didn't hear yourself verbally decide, for example, "I will be mad at her" or "I am afraid to do that"—but you actually *are* feeling that way.

How Your Experiences Create Neural Trails

Your feelings are unique. You turn on your happy chemicals with unique neural pathways built from your individual experience. That's why we react differently to the same situation even though we are all reacting with the same basic survival equipment.

Building Individual Trails

Happy moments in your past connected neurons that are there, ready to spark more happy chemicals the next time you're in similar circumstances. Unhappy moments in your past connected neurons that are there telling you what to avoid.

Each time you have an experience, your senses take in the world and trigger electricity in your brain. That electricity flows in your brain like water flows in a storm—it finds the paths of least resistance. The paths you've already built give your electricity a place to flow, and that shapes your response to the experience.

Neurochemicals pave these pathways the way asphalt paves a dirt road. Repetition also paves your pathways. Some of your neural trails develop into superhighways because you've activated them repeatedly and neurochemically. For example, a child who gets a lot of respect when she fixes her parents' computer builds a pathway that expects more good feelings when she does more to help people with computers. So she repeats the behavior, and the pathway builds. We end up with billions of pathways to channel our electricity, and they allow us to create meaning from the flood of inputs reaching our senses.

Your Neural Guidance System

The trails you have built thus far in your life combine to make up your neural guidance system. The system might not be what you'd design today if you started from scratch, but it guides your reactions to the situations you encounter on a daily basis. Your inner mammal has no reason to doubt its own reactions because they're built from your actual life experiences. You don't notice your neural guidance system because you built it without conscious intent. That's why it's hard to build new trails: You don't know how you built the old ones.

Familiar Neural Pathways Are Easy to Travel . . . but That's Not Always Good

Your neural pathways make it easy for you to like some things and dislike others. You may find yourself liking things that are not especially good for you and fearing things that actually are good for you. Why would a brain that evolved for survival build such quirky circuits?

Because we're designed to store experiences, not to delete them. Most of the time, experience holds important lessons. It helps you go toward whatever helped in the past and avoid whatever hurt. But the pathways of past experience can also mislead. They can lead you to avoid hurts that are long gone, or to seek too much of a good thing. For example, you might avoid math because a kid laughed at you in math class long ago, or you might overindulge in pizza because your parent showed kindness while sharing a pizza long ago.

Your human cortex can adjust your old circuits with new inputs: You can tackle math or resist pizza. But your old circuits are very efficient. You tend to rely on them because the world overwhelms you with information and your superhighways help it flow so well.

But those superhighways don't always take you where you want to go. Sometimes they lead you to unhappy chemicals just when you were hoping to feel good. You can enjoy more happy chemicals if you blaze new trails through your jungle of neurons. It may be harder than you expect, but it's easier when you know your equipment.

How Can You Build New Pathways?

When you were young, you built new circuits easily. In adulthood, building a new circuit is as hard as slashing through a dense rainforest. Every step requires huge effort, and the new trail you worked so hard for disappears into the undergrowth if you don't use it again soon. All this slashing may feel like a waste of time when you already have a network of superhighways to use instead.

Your neurons have difficulty sending electricity down a path you've never activated before. Each time a pathway is activated, it fires more easily. Repetition develops a neural trail slowly, the way a dirt path hardens from years of use. So how can you build new pathways? The answer is simple: Feed your brain new experiences again and again. Repetition will build the circuits you want. No one can build them for you, and you cannot build them for someone else. This book helps you select new experiences that stimulate happy chemicals, and repeat them until they surge with electricity. You can feel good in ways that are good for you.

The Vicious Cycle of Seeking Happiness

You might wish to escape unhappiness forever, but it's useful to know that unhappy chemicals are as essential to your survival as happy chemicals. Your brain needs unhappy chemicals to call attention to threats and obstacles, just as it needs happy chemicals to call attention to opportunities. You are designed to survive by seeking happy chemicals and avoiding unhappy chemicals. You are not designed for shortcuts that eliminate the seeking and avoiding. Let's see how these shortcuts can cause a vicious cycle.

Your Brain's Quest to Feel Good

The quest for good feelings is nature's survival engine. Animals seek food to relieve the bad feeling of hunger. They seek warmth to relieve the bad feeling of cold. Happy chemicals start flowing before a mammal even eats or warms up because the mammal brain turns them on as soon as it sees a way to meet a need. The human brain does this with the added boost of a cortex that makes long chains of associations. We avoid hunger by planting food and avoid chill by stocking fuel. We anticipate bad feelings in order to prevent them. But unhappy chemicals persist no matter how well you meet your needs, because your survival is threatened as long as you're alive.

A mammal risks getting eaten by a predator when it forages for food. It risks social conflict when it seeks a mate, and it risks genetic annihilation if it avoids that conflict entirely. The mammal brain never stops scanning for potential threats. When you're safe from physical threats, your brain scans for social threats. Mammals survive because the bad feeling of cortisol alerts you in time to avoid potential threats.

Cortisol communicates pain and the expectation of pain. It motivates you to do whatever it takes to make the bad feeling stop. When a lunching gazelle smells a lion, cortisol motivates it to run even though it would rather keep eating. Gazelles survive because smelling a lion feels worse than hunger. Our ancestors survived because cortisol directed their attention to one threat after another.

Your Response to Cortisol Alarms

When your cortisol surges, you respond by noticing what it's paired with. It could be low blood sugar, or the scent of danger, or social isolation. Life experience builds myriad circuits that light up when your cortisol turns on. Sometimes the solution is obvious, like pulling your hand off a hot stove. But often, you're not sure what triggered the alarm. You don't know how to make it stop, yet it feels like something awful will happen if you don't "do something" immediately. For example, let's say you have a bad feeling about your boss while sitting at your desk in your office. You want to make that feeling go away because cortisol annoys you until you do something to make it stop. But you're not sure what started it or how you can relieve it. You do know, from life experience, that doughnuts make you feel good. Doughnuts trigger happy chemicals because fat and sugar are scarce in nature. The good feeling distracts you from the bad feeling, which makes it seem like the threat is gone for the moments you are eating the doughnut. Consciously, you know the doughnut hasn't fixed your problems, but happy chemicals are molecules that pave a neural pathway. The next time you feel bad about your boss, electricity trickles to the thought of eating a doughnut. If you eat one, you build the connection. You still know the doughnut doesn't solve your problem and in fact could make it worse. But going with the flow gives you a sense of safety for that moment. When the "do something" feeling strikes, your brain builds the idea that eating a doughnut is doing something.

Chemical Ups and Downs

It would be nice to stop cortisol with permanent solutions to every problem. But that cannot happen because disappointment triggers cortisol too. When a lion loses sight of the gazelle she was stalking, her cortisol turns on. When a monkey can't crack open the nut he is working on, his cortisol turns on. Your cortisol helps you make course corrections on the path to meeting your needs. Cortisol alerts you when Plan A doesn't work.

When Plan A works, alas, the happy chemicals don't last. To get more, you have to do more. That is how a brain keeps prodding a body to do what it takes to keep its DNA alive. Happy chemicals get reabsorbed and your awareness of survival threats resumes. A "do something" feeling gets your attention when you're not distracted by happy chemicals. As you look for ways to relieve it—fast—easy happy-chemical activators may tempt you.

"Everything I like is illegal, immoral, or fattening." The old saying has some truth to it because everything that triggers fast, easy happy chemicals has side effects. Good feelings were naturally selected because of their side effects. Food evolved to feel good because that motivates a body to do what it takes to find nutrition. Sex evolved to feel good because that motivates a body to do what it takes to find a mate. The side effects of food and sex were desirable in a world of scarcity. We did not evolve to get an instant high from food and sex in every moment. Seeking a constant high can lead to a vicious cycle.

Common Vicious Cycles

 Happiness happens when these chemicals are triggered.

 Your triggers depend on the neural circuits you built in the past.

 Unhappy chemicals are always being triggered too.

 Happy chemicals distract you from the unhappy ones.

 The good feeling tempts you to activate a circuit again and again.

 Side effects result, and trigger more unhappy chemicals.

 More happy circuits are the answer. Here's how to build them.

Vicious cycles are everywhere:

- They might involve external things like alcohol, food, money, sex, and drugs.
- Or they might just be internal thought habits, like getting angry, seeking approval, escaping, thrill-seeking, and rescuing.

Each of these behaviors can make you feel good in a moment when you were feeling bad. That gives you a nice sense of conquering a threat, so you repeat the behavior. Over time, a neural superhighway develops, and the behavior seems to light up effortlessly. But side effects accumulate and trigger unhappy chemicals. Now you're even more motivated to trigger happy chemicals in the way you expect them to work. But it's like driving with one foot on the accelerator and one on the brake—the same behavior triggering both happiness and unhappiness.

How to Stop Vicious Cycles

You can stop a vicious cycle in one instant. Just resist that "do something" feeling and live with the cortisol. This is difficult to do because cortisol screams for your attention. It didn't evolve for you to sit around and accept it, after all. But you can build the skill of doing nothing during a cortisol alert, even as it begs you to make it go away by doing something. Waiting gives your brain a chance to activate an alternative. A virtuous circle starts in that moment.

Seizing the moment is easier if you have an alternative circuit ready. Your new circuit may feel awkward at first. It lacks the zip of electricity you've relied on for the sense that you know what's going on. Resisting an old circuit can make you feel like you're threatening your own survival when you're doing precisely the opposite.

The pain of resisting a habit eases once a new habit forms. You can do that in forty-five days if you repeat a new thought or behavior every day without fail. If you miss a day, start over with Day One. The new choice will not make you happy on Day One, and it may not make you happy on Day Forty. Even on Day Forty-Five, it cannot trigger happy chemicals constantly. But it will invite enough electricity to free you from a vicious cycle.

Don't Ask Your Brain for Something It Can't Give You

It's not easy being a mammal with a big cortex. We have enough neurons to imagine things that don't exist instead of just focusing on what is. This gives us the power to imagine solutions before it's too late. We improve our lives, but we also stimulate bad feelings. To feel better, we imagine a "better world," where happiness flows effortlessly and bad feelings are eradicated. But this is not a realistic expectation with the brain we have. Your brain only releases happy chemicals when you take steps toward meeting needs. You can end up in a vicious cycle if you focus on the short-run good feeling of an imagined world and neglect the reality of the world you live in.

FOCUS ON YOUR OWN PATHWAYS

It's easy to see vicious cycles in others. That's why we're tempted to take charge of other people's happiness. But you cannot reach into someone else's brain and make new connections for them, nor can they do that for you. If you focus on other people's brains, you may fail to make them happy and fail to make yourself happy. Each person must manage his or her own limbic system.

Modern society is not the cause of vicious cycles. Our ancestors had variations of their own. For example, they made human sacrifices to relieve threatened feelings, and when they felt bad again, they made more sacrifices. We have developed better ways to feel good, but side effects still plague us, so we strive to do better.

What about Love?

You've probably heard that love is the key to happiness, but it's useful to know how happy chemicals create that feeling. Love is a huge surge of happy chemicals because it's hugely relevant to the survival of your genes. You're not thinking about your genes when you're in love, but your genes are inherited from people who did what it took to reproduce successfully. Brains that motivate reproductive behavior end up making more copies of themselves. Sex is only a small part of the story. Everything from competing for healthy mates to nurturing healthy offspring is relevant to what biologists call "reproductive success." Love motivates all of these behaviors.

You may find it hard to link your loving feelings to natural selection. But in the animal world, it's easy to see how brain chemicals shape mating behavior. The mammal brain is very focused on reproductive success. Once a mammal's immediate survival needs are met, its thoughts turn to the survival of its genes. Animals are surprisingly picky about their mates. For example, every species avoids in-breeding in one way or another. Without conscious concern for genes, neurochemicals motivate alternative choices. Brains that produced in-breeders died out, while brains that motivated alternative mating choices flourished.

Love Is a Cocktail of Brain Chemicals

Each happy chemical rewards love in a different way. The familiar joys and sorrows of love are curiously equivalent to the impulses of dopamine, oxytocin, serotonin, endorphin, and cortisol. (The sex hormones, like testosterone and estrogen, are central to the feelings we associate with love, but they are outside the scope of this book because they do not trigger the feeling of happiness. They mediate specific physical responses instead.)

Dopamine

Dopamine is stimulated by the "chase" aspect of love. It's also triggered in a baby who hears his mother's footsteps. Dopamine is the brain's signal that a need is about to be met. Female chimpanzees are known to be partial to males who share their meat after a hunt. Protein is scarce in the rainforest and females need a lot of it for gestation and lactation, so meat is a great dopamine stimulator. For humans, finding "the One" makes you high on dopamine. However you define what you seek, dopamine excites you when you approach it.

Oxytocin

Oxytocin is stimulated by touch and by trust. In animals, touch and trust go together. Apes only allow trusted companions to touch them because they know from experience that violence can erupt in an instant. In humans, everything from holding hands to feeling supported triggers oxytocin. Orgasm does too. Sex triggers a lot of oxytocin at once, yielding a lot of social trust for a very short time. Holding hands stimulates a small amount of oxytocin, but when repeated over time, as in the case of an elderly couple, it builds up a circuit that easily triggers social trust. Childbirth triggers a huge oxytocin spurt in mammals, both mother and child. Nurturing other people's children can stimulate it too. Friendship bonds stimulate oxytocin, and they also promote reproductive success. Monkeys and apes with more social alliances have more surviving offspring, and adolescents clearly desire individuals with more social alliances too. Oxytocin is related to love in so many ways that it is often called the bonding hormone or the cuddle chemical.

Serotonin

Serotonin is stimulated by the status aspect of love—the pride of associating with a person of a certain stature. You may hate thinking of your love in this way, but you can easily see it in others. Animals with higher status in their social groups have more reproductive success, and natural selection built a brain that rewards you with the good feeling of serotonin when you raise your status. This may be hard to believe, but research on a huge range of species shows tremendous energy invested in the pursuit of status. Social dominance leads to more mating opportunity and more surviving offspring—and it feels good. We no longer try to survive by having as many offspring as possible, but when you receive the affection of someone you perceive as important, your serotonin surges.

Endorphin

Endorphin is stimulated by physical pain, but you get a bit from laughing and crying too. Lovers are known for laughing together, and it's interesting to know that they are stimulating each other's endorphin. Crying is associated with love too, alas. Confusing love and pain is a bad survival strategy, but endorphin pathways may explain some people's tolerance for painful relationships.

Cortisol

Cortisol plays an important role in reproductive success, too. It makes you feel bad when you lose love, which promotes survival by helping you move on. If you remained attached to a person who is not available to you, your genes would be doomed. Cortisol helps your brain rewire to associate your old lover with negative rather than positive expectations, so you start seeking love elsewhere. We wish lost love wouldn't feel so bad, but it's interesting to know that the bad feeling has a valuable function.

In animals, it's easy to see how bad feelings promote love:

- Cortisol motivates a mammal mama to guard her child constantly and to search for nourishment to sustain her milk.
- Cortisol motivates a male mammal to avoid conflicts he's likely to lose and to risk conflicts he's likely to win. If your social standing is threatened, cortisol alarms you because lost status threatens your DNA in the state of nature.

The Ups and Downs of Love and Survival

Love feels bad for a subtle reason that's widely overlooked. We are born helpless and need love to survive. The first experience in each brain is the sensation of needs that you cannot meet for yourself. You feel good when others meet your needs, and you come to expect that. Alas, we must transition from childlike dependence to mature independence. That can feel like a survival threat to the part of your brain that expects to be taken care of. This motivates people to find adult love, and that keeps our genes alive. But the interdependence of mature love never measures up to the dependence of your brain's first circuits.

Love feels good because it's hard to keep your DNA alive in the state of nature. Survival rates are low and mating opportunities are harder to come by than you might expect. Without a huge effort, your genes would get wiped off the face of the earth. Now, I know you are not thinking about your genes, and animals aren't either. But every brain is inherited from individuals who did what it took to reproduce. Love makes it feel good.

There is no free love in nature. Every species has preliminary qualifying events before mating. Creatures work hard for any mating opportunity that comes their way. Good feelings reward you for pursuing the quest. Bad feelings warn you that your genes will be annihilated if you don't get busy. Something as small as failing to get a smile from the person you smile at can trigger surprising neurochemistry because your brain relates it to the survival prospects of your genes.

In modern times, people want romantic love throughout their lives, but expectations were different in the past. Children started coming as soon as you had sex, and they cried if you didn't keep feeding them. You were too busy to worry about romantic love. If you lived to middle age, you had grandchildren with more needs. People had the same basic neurochemistry, but without birth control they were more focused on immediate survival. Today, we explore many ways to trigger happy chemicals, but you must keep working to keep them coming. Each burst of a happy chemical is metabolized in a short time so you're always looking for ways to get more. Maybe that's why love songs are always popular. They stimulate brain chemicals without the messy side effects.

And now let's meet those happy chemicals in more detail.

2 | MEET YOUR HAPPY CHEMICALS

You're Unique . . . but You're Human

Your feelings are unique, but the chemicals that cause your feelings are the same as everyone else's.

Your life experience is unique, but it overlaps with everyone's because the same basic survival needs command your brain's attention.

You may say you're not focused on your "survival," and you may not be, consciously. Loftier goals such as world peace and social justice get your attention when you talk to yourself in words. But your happy chemicals respond to your mammalian survival prospects as your brain has learned to define them.

Meet Your Dopamine

Dopamine promotes survival by telling your body where to invest its energy. Your ancestors foraged for food by walking slowly until something triggered their excitement. That dopamine told them when to go for it. The mammal brain scans constantly for potential rewards, and dopamine is the signal that it has found some. It feels good, which motivates you to keep seeking and finding.

It's important to understand foraging to understand your brain. Our ancestors didn't know where their next meal was coming from. They constantly scanned their surroundings for something that looked good, and then invested energy in pursuit. Dopamine is at the core of this process. In today's world, you don't need to forage for food, but dopamine makes you feel good when you scan your world, find evidence of something that felt good before, and go for it. You are constantly deciding what is worth your effort and when it's better to conserve your effort. Your dopamine circuits guide that decision. You might wish the good feeling of dopamine just flowed all the time, but that wouldn't really benefit you.

When Do You Feel Dopamine?

A marathon runner gets a surge of dopamine when she sees the finish line. A football player is fueled by dopamine when he scores and does a victory dance. "I did it!" the brain tells the body. It feels so good that you look for ways to trigger that feeling again.

Of course, dopamine didn't evolve for crossing arbitrary lines on the ground. It evolved to release energy when you have a chance to meet a survival need. An ape climbing to a piece of fruit enjoys dopamine as she nears the reward. Dopamine releases her reserve tank of energy so she's able to meet her needs. She doesn't say "I did it!" in words, but neurochemicals create that feeling without words.

An ape's dopamine starts flowing as soon as she sees a fruit she can reach. That's because her brain built a dopamine pathway when she first tasted fruit. The sugar triggered the message "this meets your needs! Get more of it!" That dopamine surge connected all the neurons active at that moment, which wired her dopamine to turn on when she sees anything similar in the future.

How You Built Dopamine Circuits

Your dopamine circuits are built from your own past dopamine experiences. Imagine a child foraging with his mother. He sees her excitement when they stumble on a delicious berry patch. His mirror neurons (which mirror the behavior of others, as we'll learn more about in Chapter 3) get his dopamine flowing before he ever eats a berry. When he has his first taste, flavors rare in nature get his attention. More dopamine is triggered, which paves a pathway to the neurons active at that moment. That will help him recognize sights, sounds, and smells associated with berries in the future.

Without effort or intent, dopamine builds a neural template that helps you find rewards. It also stimulates the energy you need to pursue rewards. We are not born with circuits defining the rewards that meet our needs. We build them from life experience. That's why one person gets excited about eating crickets while another person gets excited about the Food Network. You can meet your needs by foraging for a career opportunity rather than a berry patch. But you do it with the operating system that met survival needs before there was language.

Dopamine's Ups and Downs

You may not have a "Wow!" feeling about berries, because sweetness is no longer a rare taste. Your brain saves your energy for rewards that are scarce in your life experience. I get a rush of excitement when I see the first cherries of the season, but my excitement doesn't last. Looking at cherries can't make me happy all the time. My brain saves its dopamine for things relevant to my present needs instead of wasting it on things already available.

Social rewards are not easily available because they can't be mass produced like berries and sugar. Seeking and finding social rewards stimulates the excitement of dopamine. People invest years of effort trying to become a heart surgeon or a rock star because each step along the way triggers dopamine. Even if your goal is committing the perfect crime or living on the beach, your brain releases dopamine as you seek and find steps that bring you closer. The social rewards that stimulate your dopamine depend on your unique life experience. But we all live with the fact that dopamine is soon metabolized and you have to approach a reward again to get more.

Research on Dopamine

The fleetingness of dopamine was illuminated by a land-mark monkey study. The animals were trained to do a task and get rewarded with spinach. After a few days, they were rewarded with squirts of juice instead of spinach. This was a bigger reward than they expected and the monkeys' dopamine soared. But as the experimenters continued rewarding with juice, the monkeys' dopamine declined to nothing in a few days. Their brains stopped reacting to the sweet, juicy reward. In human terms, they took it for granted. Dopamine evolved to store new information about rewards. When there's no new information, there's no need for dopamine.

This experiment has a dramatic finale. The experimenters switched back to spinach, and the monkeys reacted with fits of rage. They screamed and threw the spinach back at the research-ers. The monkeys had learned to expect juice. It no longer made them happy, but losing it made them mad.

THE CONNECTION BETWEEN COCAINE AND DOPAMINE

Cocaine stimulates more dopamine than real life. It gives you the thrill of finding berries or finishing a marathon without leaving the couch. You get the excitement of accomplishment without having to accomplish anything. Natural rewards feel less exciting if your brain learns to expect an artificial jolt.

Such research improves our understanding of dopamine sig-nificantly over initial research conducted in the 1950s. You have probably heard about the rat wired up to electrically stimulate its "pleasure center" by pressing a lever. The rat seized the day, press-ing constantly until it dropped dead. It would not stop for food or water or attractive mates. Scientists presumed the electrode was triggering pleasure. But why would a brain define pleasure in a way that motivated it to die rather than eat, drink, or mate? Now we realize that the *expectation* of reward triggers dopamine. The unfortunate rat kept expecting rewards from the lever because it triggered more dopamine than real-world rewards.

Dopamine and Survival

A small potential reward triggers a small surge of dopamine; a huge potential reward triggers a huge surge of dopamine. For example, mothers have been seen lifting a car when their child is pinned underneath. Saving your child's life is the biggest reward there is from the perspective of your genes. A mother is not consciously thinking of her genes when she risks her life to save her child; she's not thinking at all. Such mothers report they had no idea what they were doing. The verbal part of the brain is not needed for a dopamine circuit to unleash the energy needed for the job.

The link between dopamine and survival is not always obvious, however. For example, computer games stimulate dopamine, even though they don't meet real needs. Computer games reward you with points that your mind has linked to social rewards. To get the points, you activate the seek-and-find mechanism that evolved for foraging. You keep enjoying dopamine as you keep approaching rewards. The dopamine paves a pathway that tells you to expect good feelings from computer games. The next time you feel bad, the game is one way your brain knows to relieve those bad feelings. From your mammal brain's perspective, it relieves the threat, though the social rewards may prove more elusive.

EXERCISE: WHEN DO YOU FEEL DOPAMINE?

Dopamine is the excitement you feel when you expect a reward. A hungry lion expects a reward when she sees an isolated gazelle. A thirsty elephant expects a reward when he sees signs of a water hole. Dopamine unleashes your reserve tank of energy when you see a way to meet a need. Even when you're just sitting still, dopamine motivates you to scan a lot of detail to find a pattern that's somehow relevant to your needs. When you find details that are "just right," it feels good. Finding the puzzle piece you're looking for feels good because of dopamine.

Whatever triggered your dopamine when you were young paved neural pathways that tell your dopamine when to turn on today. These circuits work without words, so your dopamine can be hard to make sense of. You will learn if you pay close attention to patterns in your excitement. Sometimes this is easier to see in others (though they may not appreciate your observations). Spend time noticing the joy of finding what you seek:

In your work

_____

_____

_____

In your free time

_____

_____

_____

In someone else

_____

_____

_____

In surprise rewards you weren't looking for

_____

_____

_____

The Quest for "More"

The urge for more did not start with "our society." In fact, our ancestors never stopped seeking either. When their bellies were full, they looked for new ways to meet their needs by making better arrows and stronger shelters. We know how hard they searched for the right materials because archaeological sites often contain materials from far away. Dopamine made the quest feel good, but the feeling soon passed and they kept seeking more. Every brain learns to link effort and reward, whether material rewards, social rewards, or relief from a threat.

If you are studying for a math test, you are fueled by dopamine. You may not consciously think it feels good, but something in your life connected math to other rewards. It could be material rewards, social rewards, or just the good feeling of an achievement. Solving math problems is another kind of seek-and-find activity. When you find the right answer, you get that "I did it!" feeling, which erases any cortisol feelings for a moment. When your answer is wrong, you may try again because you still expect a reward.

An athlete spends long hours training because a little dopamine is stimulated by each step toward expected rewards. Winning games or medals triggers a big burst of dopamine, but these are only steps as well. An athlete has linked these steps to rewards that feel relevant to survival, be it material rewards, social rewards, or internal rewards.

Each brain has built expectations about survival rewards and the steps it takes to reach them. When you moved toward your expected reward, dopamine makes it feel good.

Meet Your Endorphin

"Euphoria" is a common description of the endorphin feeling. But this neurochemical did not evolve for good times. Physical pain is what triggers it. You may have taken a bad fall and got up thinking you were fine, only to discover that you're seriously injured. That's the power of endorphin.

Endorphin masks pain for a short time, which promotes survival by giving an injured mammal a chance to reach safety. If your ancestor broke his leg while hunting, or got worn down by hunger and thirst, the oblivion of endorphin helped him do what it took to save himself.

"Runner's high" is a well-known endorphin experience. But you cannot get a daily high from a daily run. Endorphin is only released if you push past your capacity to the point of distress. This is not necessarily a good way to promote survival. Endorphin did not evolve to motivate self-inflicted pain. It evolved to escape pain.

Perhaps you've seen a zebra wriggle out of the jaws of a lion on a wildlife documentary. You see the zebra's flesh ripped open but it can still run. Endorphin masks the pain for a few moments, which helps the zebra escape. If it fails to escape and ends up in the lion's jaw, it will at least die in an endorphin haze. It's nice to know about nature's morphine when you see disturbing footage. It reminds you that endorphin exists not for partying but for momentary respite in the struggle for life.

Pain Does Have Value

The respite of endorphin is brief because pain has survival value. Pain is your body's signal that something is urgently wrong. If you ignored pain all the time, you would touch hot stoves and walk on broken legs. You would not make good survival choices if you were always high on endorphin. We evolved to notice distress signals, not to keep masking them with oblivion.

When endorphin was discovered, it was called endogenous morphine because it was so similar to opiates yet was produced by the body's own endogenous systems. But it would be more true to say that morphine is the drug industry's endorphin. Heroin and other opium derivatives have an effect on us because they fit our natural endorphin receptors.

We are not designed to release endorphin all the time. Exercise can give you a little, but exercising to the point of pain doesn't promote survival. Laughing and crying trigger internal convulsions that stimulate endorphin, but this road to euphoria is limited too. Fake laughs don't trigger the internal convulsions, and real laughs only last for seconds. Real cries are painful, and fake cries don't trigger the physical distress.

A broken heart doesn't trigger endorphin the way a broken bone does. Endorphin did not evolve to mask social pain. In the past, daily life held so much physical pain that social pain was secondary. Today, we suffer less from the pain of manual labor, predator attack, foraging accidents, and deteriorating disease. We have more energy to focus on painful social disappointments. This leaves us feeling that life is more painful even as it's less painful.

EXERCISE: WHEN DO YOU FEEL ENDORPHIN?

Endorphin is an oblivious feeling that masks physical pain. Endorphin allows an injured animal to escape from a predator and save its life. We are designed for survival, not for getting high. Nature's opiate is only released in short spurts because pain is actually good for you: it tells you not to touch fire or run on a broken leg. Exercise is good, but "runner's high" only happens if you exercise to the point of pain. We are not designed to inflict pain on ourselves to feel good. Fortunately, small drips of endorphin are stimulated by laughing, crying, and reasonable exertion. You can't expect a constant high, but you can celebrate your body's ability to manage pain. Notice your endorphin at work in a moment when:

You were hurt but didn't realize it for a few minutes

_____

_____

_____

You felt good after a big physical exertion

_____

_____

_____

You felt good after a belly laugh

_____

_____

_____

You felt good after a real cry

_____

_____

_____

Adrenaline Is Not the Same As Endorphin

Endorphin is different from adrenaline. Skydiving and bungee jumping trigger an "adrenaline high." You anticipate pain and your body releases adrenaline to handle the emergency. The "adrenaline junkie" is not seeking pain, but the rush of energy designed to avoid pain. When you see the ground rushing at you, your brain anticipates pain, even if you're safely attached to a rope or a roller coaster. Your brain evolved in a world of real threats, not self-imposed, artificially concocted threats.

Adrenaline is outside the scope of this book because it does not cause happiness. It causes a state of arousal, as if your body is stepping on the gas. Some people learn to like that feeling, but it is not a signal that something is good for you.

It is a signal that something is extremely relevant to survival, whether good or bad, and thus requires your energy. For example, if you are about to accept the Nobel Prize from the king of Sweden, a spurt of adrenaline tells you that the moment is important and provides the energy to manage it. If your parachute doesn't open, that is important too. Adrenaline amplifies the positive or negative message conveyed by the other neurochemicals. It prepares you for immediate action, but it doesn't tell you whether that action should be going toward or running away.

Meet Your Oxytocin

When you feel like you can lean on someone, oxytocin creates that feeling. When you trust someone, or enjoy someone's trust in you, oxytocin is flowing. The pleasure of belonging or safety in numbers is oxytocin too.

The Connection Between Oxytocin and Trust

Social trust promotes survival, so the brain rewards it with a good feeling. But trusting everyone is not good for survival. That's why your brain evolved to analyze social alliances instead of just releasing oxytocin all the time.

Feeding a horse is a simple example of the oxytocin feeling. When I walk toward a horse with food in my hand, we check each other out. The horse fears strangers but wants the food. I fear putting my hand into those huge teeth but I want to enjoy the shared trust. Each of us scans for evidence that it's safe to trust. When both of us are satisfied that the other doesn't pose an immediate threat, we relax, and it feels good. That's the release of oxytocin.

Horses survive by trusting their herd mates. A herd is an extended alarm system. Each horse shares the burden of staying alert for predators. The horse that trusts its fellow horses can relax a bit and still survive.

Mammals live in herds and packs and troops because there's safety in numbers. If they are separated from their group mates, their oxytocin falls and they feel bad. A herd animal panics when it can't see at least one of its group. When it rejoins them, a surge of oxytocin relieves the cortisol.

Oxytocin and Reproduction

Mammals take the risk of leaving their group when it promotes reproduction. Young mammals transfer to a new troop at puberty to improve mating opportunities. (Depending on the species, either the males or the females disperse at puberty.) A mother mammal leaves her group to search for a lost child or to give birth. Reproductive behaviors trigger more oxytocin than mere companionship, which motivates a mammal to leave the group to promote its genes.

When a mammal gives birth, her oxytocin surges. This motivates her to guard the newborn constantly in addition to facilitating labor and lactation. Oxytocin spikes in the newborn brain too, so a young mammal clings to its mother without comprehending the danger of leaving her. When the birth process is over, more oxytocin is stimulated by holding or licking. This paves neural pathways that facilitate the flow of oxytocin in similar settings. Bonds of attachment are a buildup of oxytocin circuits. Over time, attachment extends from the mother to the herd or pack or troop.

Touch triggers oxytocin. Primates are often seen running their fingers through a troop mate's fur to remove debris. Oxytocin makes it feel good to both the giver and the receiver. Monkeys and apes invest a lot of time grooming others, and it appears to establish social alliances. Researchers find that monkeys and apes with more social alliances get better mating opportunities and have more surviving offspring. When there's a conflict in a troop, primates tend to aid the individuals they groom with. Social alliances can entangle you in trouble, but oxytocin makes it feel good.

Trusting the Group vs. Trusting Yourself

A herd only protects you if you follow the crowd and run when they run. If you insist on seeing the lion for yourself before you run, you are less likely to survive. Natural selection built a brain that can trust the judgment of others. But herd behavior has a downside that's obvious to humans. We worry about jumping over cliffs when the other lemmings jump. We worry about group-think and gangs and codependence. We override our herd impulses and strike out on our own. But we often feel like a lamb among lions because of our urge for oxytocin.

Reptiles have no warm and fuzzy feelings toward other reptiles. They stay alone in their vigilance instead of distributing the burden among many eyes and ears. A lizard never trusts other lizards. Its chemical equivalent of oxytocin is only released during mating and egg laying.

Reptiles strike out on their own the moment they're born. Instead of relying on parental care, a young lizard starts running the instant she hatches from her shell. If she doesn't run fast enough, a parent eats her—the better to recycle the energy into another sibling instead of letting a predator get it. Fish don't even wait for their eggs to hatch. They swim off to pursue other interests the moment their eggs are fertilized. Plants send their seed into the wind without ever knowing if it grows into mighty oaks.

Mammals, on the other hand, bond with their child because oxytocin receptors prepare us to feel good about it. (Birds have some parental care too, and they have a molecular equivalent of oxytocin.) Parental attachment revolutionized the biology of the brain. It became possible for mammals to be born without survival skills and to learn from life experience instead. Unlike reptiles, fish, and plants, which are born with all necessary survival knowledge, mammals are born fragile and stupid. The mammal brain does not fully develop in the safety of the uterus or egg. It develops by interacting with the world around it. A mammal needs protection while its brain is still developing, but this investment leads to a huge advantage: Each generation wires itself to survive in the world it actually lives in rather than the world of its ancestors.

Brain Size Matters

The smaller an animal's brain, the more it relies on prewired survival skills. That prewired brain is adapted to a specific ecological niche, and it quickly dies outside that niche. The bigger an animal's brain, the more it builds survival skills from life experience. A big brain makes connections instead of being born with connections. The larger a creature's brain, the longer it remains helpless after birth. It takes time to fill a brain with useful connections.

A big brain creates a huge survival dilemma because a fragile newborn is easily eaten by predators. A big-brained baboon or elephant cannot birth hundreds of offspring for a few to survive, the way a small-brained snake or lizard does. A warm-blooded, big-brained infant is hard to gestate, so a mother can only make a few in her lifetime. If she loses them to predators, her genes are wiped out. So she does her darnedest to keep every single one alive.

Oxytocin and Attachment

But the more you invest in each child, the more you lose if it dies. Attachment is what makes this strategy work. Momma mammals guard each newborn constantly, and herds help them out. When a predator snatches a young mammal, the mother loses a chunk of her lifetime reproductive capacity, but oxytocin keeps motivating attachment.

For most of human history, people spent their lives in the network of attachments they were born into. They might have transferred to a new group to mate, but such transfers were otherwise limited. Today, lasting attachments are less preferred and often disparaged. Without them, however, we feel like something is wrong. We don't know why, but we long for the place where "everybody knows your name." Or the crowded sports arena or concert hall where thousands of people act on the same impulse. Or the political group that shares your anger. Or the online forum that welcomes your comments. These things feel good because social alliances stimulate oxytocin. Of course, they are only brief moments of trust—small squirts that will soon pass. And that's why the brain is always looking for a chance to stimulate more.

EXERCISE: WHEN DO YOU FEEL OXYTOCIN?

Oxytocin is the pleasure of letting down your guard near those you trust. It's not the conscious decision to trust, but the physical feeling of safety you get from proximity to trusted others. Oxytocin flows in a gazelle surrounded by its herd and a monkey having its fur groomed. Social alliances promote survival, and mammals evolved a brain that makes it feel good. A human brain can abstract, so we can enjoy the feeling of social support without others being physically present. Our oxytocin pathways build from life experience. We mammals surge with oxytocin at birth, which builds our core attachment circuits. We wire ourselves to trust whatever we experience while our oxytocin is flowing. That's how a young mammal transfers its attachment from its mother to its herd. Humans often leave the herd we grew up in, but our brains still crave oxytocin. Notice the good feeling stimulated by the following opportunities to lower your guard:

Someone protects or supports you

_____

_____

_____

You protect or support someone

_____

_____

_____

The touch of someone you trust

_____

_____

_____

The physical proximity of someone you trust

_____

_____

_____

Coping with Betrayed Trust

Alas, the good feeling of social trust sometimes leads to the bad feeling of betrayed trust. Since we avoid bad feelings, we make careful decisions about when to trust and when to withhold trust. Primates have enough neurons to be choosy about their friends. Monkeys and apes form individualized attachments instead of all-or-nothing bonds to a troop. With each social interaction, they update their circuits with oxytocin or cortisol. Over time, you "know who your friends are" because your neurochemicals react to individuals as "good for your survival" or "bad for your survival."

OXYTOCIN AND LONG-TERM BONDS

Monogamy is rare in the mammal world, though it appears in species with high oxytocin. Most mammals bond with foraging partners rather than sex partners. You might have mixed feelings about the people you eat with and work with. You might not trust them sometimes and even wonder why you put up with them. But when you leave them, your oxytocin falls and your mammal brain tells you that something is wrong.

Primates are always negotiating their social alliances. This is easy to see in your daily life, when you interact with family members, friends, coworkers, or neighbors. You may find it annoying when you see others do it. But when you seek support, you feel like you are just trying to survive. Social alliances transform threatened feelings into safe feelings thanks to oxytocin.

Meet Your Serotonin

Getting respect feels good because it triggers serotonin. The good feeling motivates you to seek more respect, and that promotes survival. You may feel sure that you don't think this way, but you can easily see this dynamic in others. In the animal world, getting respect clearly promotes an individual's DNA. They're not thinking about genes, of course. They seek social dominance because serotonin makes it feel good. They avoid conflict because it's linked to pain. The mammal brain is always looking for ways to enjoy the good feeling of serotonin without the bad feeling of pain.

The Connection Between Dominance and Serotonin

Each mammal species has gestures that signal dominance and submission. A dominance gesture signals the intent to control food or mating opportunity. A submission gesture protects an individual from the pain of conflict with stronger individuals. Animals only fight when both individuals believe they are stronger. Conflict is usually avoided because animals are skilled at assessing their relative strength, and the weaker individual submits to avoid harm.

In the human world, we shift fluidly between the dominant and subordinate position in the course of each day. We sustain goodwill by taking the lead sometimes and ceding control at other times. You can say no one should ever dominate, but if you collide in a doorway and say "after you," but the other person says "after you," someone must act or you'll be in that doorway forever. Maybe you will go last by insisting harder, and then feel superior about it. That's your mammal brain's quest for serotonin.

Mammals seek the one-up position because serotonin makes it feel good. One study showed this by separating an alpha vervet monkey from his troop with a one-way mirror. (An alpha is the individual to whom group mates routinely defer.) The alpha monkey made the dominance gestures typical of his species, but his subordinates did not respond with the expected submission gestures because the one-way mirror blocked their view of him. The alpha got agitated and his serotonin level fell. Each day the experiment continued, his serotonin kept dropping and his agitation grew. He needed their submission to keep up his serotonin.

Serotonin and Survival

All living creatures have serotonin, even amoeba. One-celled animals use serotonin in a way that's curiously relevant to us. We humans have more serotonin in our digestive system than we have in our brains. An amoeba is too small to have separate digestive and nervous systems, so it uses serotonin in a dual way that explains everything. Serotonin signals the amoeba's body to move toward food and get ready to digest it. The mechanism is astonishingly simple. An amoeba constantly forages and scans for danger by letting tiny amounts of water pass through its cell membrane. If the water sample shows a high concentration of foreign material, the amoeba interprets that as danger and it wiggles off in a random direction. If the sample contains a low level of foreign material, the amoeba perceives a good feeding opportunity and releases serotonin. That straightens its tail so it forges straight ahead, and it turns on its digestive juices. Serotonin is the sensation that it's safe to go ahead and meet your needs.

In mammals, serotonin is the good feeling of having secure access to food or other resources. The stronger mammals in a herd or pack or troop typically dominate food and mating opportunities. This may conflict with one's pristine view of nature, but close observation of countless species shows that each has its way of competing for resources. Much of the time, animals are having food fights, battling over mating opportunities, and doing everything possible to get their offspring ahead. Humans strive to curb these impulses, but we've inherited a brain that makes social dominance feel good. We scan for ways to enjoy the good feeling of social importance without the bad feeling of conflict.

Imagine a piglet born in a litter of sixteen to a mother who has twelve teats. Each piglet struggles for nourishment from the moment of birth. Complex decisions are required. If a piglet doesn't struggle it could starve to death, but if it struggles too much, it may get injured in conflict or simply consume more energy than it takes in. Serotonin helps a piglet find the level of assertion that's just right. Each time a piglet succeeds at dominating another, it gets a squirt of serotonin. That motivates it to seek more of the good feeling, and the extra nourishment helps it prevail. But it fails sometimes, and its serotonin falls. That motivates it to submit and conserve energy. Serotonin promotes survival whether it's up or down by balancing energy expenditure with food intake.

The piglet's cortisol spikes if it's seriously underfed. That motivates aggression, which helps it get food. Aggression is different from social dominance, because cortisol feels bad while serotonin feels good. Social dominance is the calm, secure expectation that you will get what you need. Cortisol is the sense that something awful will happen if you don't act now.

When a piglet has extra energy, it strives to dominate a teat and keep others away. If it succeeds, it strives for a better teat— one closer to the mother's heart. The top teat brings more nutrition and more warmth than the hind teats. Researchers are still debating this, but farmers have observed it for centuries.

Mother Pig does not intervene in this conflict. The siblings sort it out for themselves by the time they are a few days old. Each piglet learns from the experience of pleasure and pain. Each brain builds expectations that tell it when to forge ahead to meet its needs and when to hold back to avoid pain. Soon the piglets will be out foraging for their own food, and then start competing for mating opportunities.

Intra-Group Conflict

Every brain longs for the good feeling of serotonin, but the motivation is easier to see in others and can be difficult to see in yourself. The point is not that you should push your way to the best teat. The point is that your brain constantly monitors your access to resources. When access looks secure, you feel good for a moment, and then you look for ways to make it more secure. You may get annoyed when you see others trying to secure their position. But when you do it, you think, "I'm just trying to survive."

Securing resources is tricky for creatures that live in groups. A solitary reptile can just lunge at food without worrying about others. If a group-living mammal lunged at food, it might crash into a bigger, stronger individual who would attack it. Avoiding injury promotes survival more than any one bite of food. So the impulse to compare yourself to others and decide whether you're stronger or weaker is more pressing than the impulse to eat. When a mammal sees that it's weaker, it restrains itself until the other has eaten. When a mammal sees that it's stronger, its serotonin surges and it lunges at food.

I am not saying we should dominate the weak. I am saying we should recognize our own evolutionary urge to make social comparisons and come out on top. Young mammals quickly learn that stronger individuals will bite them if they're in the way of desirable resources. The pain of being bitten wires a youth to hold back. You may call it "cooperation" when you see an animal hold back, but the animal wants its chance to eat and reproduce. It is not lyricizing about cooperation. It is scanning for safe opportunities to go for it.

MALE VS. FEMALE SURVIVAL STRATEGIES

Each gender seeks dominance in ways that best promote its DNA. In most species, females invest so heavily in each offspring that their genes are best served by enhancing the survivability of her young. A male's reproductive success is often served by maximizing mating opportunities. Within these strategies, both genders dominate and submit to meet their needs.

Animals can't save money for a rainy day. The only way they can put something aside for the future is to invest today's extra energy into social power that can help them survive tomorrow. That's why each mammalian herd or pack or troop has its status hierarchy. The organization is not conscious, of course. Each individual simply remembers whom they fear and whom they trust, and a hierarchy emerges organically. Cortisol tells a mammal to hunch down in self-defense in the face of a stronger group mate. Serotonin tells a mammal to swell with pride (or air, depending on how you look at it) when it is strong enough to get respect and meet its needs.

A cow that pushes her way to the center of the herd is safer from predators than a cow near the edge of the herd. The pushy cow improves her chances of living to reproduce and keeping her young alive. Bulls typically avoid the herd until mating time, when they ferociously battle other males for admission. The most dominant bull pushes his way to the center of the herd, where he meets and inseminates the most dominant cows. In each species, social dominance promotes reproductive success in one way or another. I am not advocating such behavior, simply recognizing the human challenge of trying to feel good while avoiding conflict.

Are Animals Really Selfless?

You may have heard that animals are altruistic. There's a demand for evidence that nature is good, and researchers tend to supply "studies" that meet the demand. In the name of science, hundreds of trials are done, and instances that can be construed as altruism are reported. The illusion of animal altruism is often built on highly artificial laboratory scenarios. In the wild, animals will snatch food from the mouths of juveniles who dare to go for it, but that's not reported in the news.

In the animal world, higher-status males generally get more mating opportunities. Higher-status females tend to be more fertile and their young have higher survival rates. Brains that seek social dominance made more copies of themselves. We are descended from them.

At the same time, we strive for social trust to stimulate oxytocin. Your brain is always looking for ways to enjoy serotonin without losing oxytocin or increasing cortisol. For example, if your comment in a meeting gets respect, that feels good. But if you dominate the meeting, you may end up with pain. Each experience of pain or pleasure builds connections that help you figure out how to feel good and survive. Your brain is always trying to get respect using the circuits you have. (This is the subject of my book *I, Mammal: Why Your Brain Links Status and Happiness*.)

EXERCISE: WHEN DO YOU FEEL SEROTONIN?

Serotonin is the feeling of being important. We see how much others like to feel important, but we hate to see this in ourselves. It helps to know that our brain was naturally selected to seek social dominance, because brains that did so made more copies of their genes. We strive to avoid conflict because aggression can wipe out your genes. So the mammal brain keeps calculating social data, and when you find a safe way to assert yourself, it rewards you with serotonin. A big human cortex tries to stimulate serotonin with abstractions rather than one-on-one showdowns, such as "pride," "confidence," or "self-respect." It feels good ... even if you hate to admit it. Noticing your mammalian urge for serotonin is a valuable skill. Practice by looking for:

Someone you don't like seeking importance

_____

_____

_____

Someone you like seeking importance

_____

_____

_____

A moment when you feel respected

_____

_____

_____

A moment when you enjoy a competitive edge

_____

_____

_____

It's All Relative

Your past serotonin experiences built circuits that create your present expectations. If you expect to be master of the universe, you may end up feeling disrespected much of the time. Your life may be fine in objective terms, but the expectation of continual admiration from others leads to disappointment. A person who has set her sights differently may feel satisfied with the respect she is getting from her world, and thus enjoy the calm, secure feeling of serotonin.

Social dominance is different from socioeconomic status. A person who is number 3 on the world billionaire list might feel like his survival is threatened when he falls to number 4. By contrast, a person with little socioeconomic status might harshly dominate those around him and feel good about it.

Many social dominance strategies are unrelated to formal wealth and status. Appearance is a good example. One person may feel respected for his appearance, while another feels disrespected, even if the two people look exactly the same. Our neurochemicals depend on the expectation circuits we've built.

Antidepressants, like Prozac, are known for raising serotonin levels in the brain. The function of serotonin was not understood when antidepressants were introduced to the public, in the same way that aspirin was used before anyone knew how it worked. They may have created the impression that ingesting some "correct level" of serotonin can make a person happy independent of their thoughts and actions. We are only at the first stages of understanding the link between serotonin and happiness. Animals offer insight into our neurochemical ups and downs, but these insights are unsettling. The dominance-seeking urges of mammals are not a prescription for happiness, but they are a window into the power of self-respect.

Each happy chemical turns on for a specific survival reason, and then turns off so it's ready to alert you to another survival opportunity. Unhappy chemicals are less noticeable during a happy spurt, but they get your attention when the spurt fades. It would be nice to eliminate unhappy chemicals, but the following chapter explains why they're here to stay.

3 | WHY YOUR BRAIN CREATES UNHAPPI-NESS

Unhappy Chemicals Are Nature's Security Alarm

When you see a lizard basking in the sun, you might think it's the picture of serenity. But in truth, that lizard is just trying to avoid death. Cold-blooded reptiles die of hypothermia unless they sun themselves often, but when they're out in the sun, they risk being eaten alive by a predator. So a lizard shuttles constantly between the lethal threats of sun and shade. He makes these decisions by literally running from bad feelings.

He runs to the sun when a drop in body temperature caused his cortisol to surge. Once he's exposed and vulnerable in the sun, he scans constantly for predators and runs at the slightest whiff of harm. He is not having fun. But he survives because his brain is skilled at weighing one threat against another.

The human brain stem and cerebellum are eerily similar to a reptile's brain. Nature adapts old parts rather than starting over. We still use the reptile brain for the jobs it is good at, like metabolic balance and alerting to potential harm. Mammals added a layer onto the reptile brain that makes social life possible, and humans added on a layer that matches patterns among the past, present, and future. Your reptile brain lies where these higher layers and your body intersect, so it's not surprising that you find patterns in the social world that give your body a threatened feeling. Many people end up feeling threatened more than they'd like to, so it helps to know how your threat detector works.

How Cortisol Works

Cortisol is your body's emergency broadcast system. Corticoid hormones are produced by reptiles, amphibians, fish, and even worms, when they encounter survival threats. It creates the feeling humans call "pain." Pain gets your attention. It feels bad because that works—it focuses your attention on whatever it takes to make it stop. The brain strives to avoid pain by storing details of the experience so you know what to look out for in the future. When you see things associated with past pain, your cortisol starts flowing so you can act in time to avoid future pain. A big brain can generate many associations, so it can anticipate many possible sources of pain.

When cortisol surges, we call it "fear," but when cortisol dribbles, we call it "anxiety" or "stress." These bad feelings tell you that pain will come if you don't act fast. Your reptile brain can't say why it released the cortisol. Electricity just flowed down a pathway. When you understand how this happens, you can distinguish more easily between internal alarms and external threats.

You might think you'd be free from cortisol if the world were in better shape. But your brain sees every disappointment as a threat, and this response has value. It alerts you in time to prevent further setbacks and disappointments. For example, if you've walked miles to get water and realize you're on the wrong trail, a surge of bad feeling protects you from walking any farther on the wrong trail. You cannot make perfect predictions all the time, so your cortisol will always have a job to do. Understanding your cortisol helps you make peace with the world around you.

Cortisol Wires to Whatever Precedes Pain

The sensory inputs you experience just before a moment of pain are essential information from a survival perspective. They enable you to recognize trouble before it happens. The brain stores such information without conscious effort or intent because sensory inputs remain electrically active for a moment before they extinguish. This "buffer memory" allows pain circuits to include the events that preceded the pain. They enable creatures to detect probable threats without need for rational analysis.

Sometimes, the brain wires in quirky associations between pain and the moments before pain. For example, there was a girl who panicked when she heard laughter. The girl had been in a car crash that killed some of her friends. She awoke from a coma without remembering the accident, and began having panic attacks at the sound of laughter. A therapist helped her remember that she was laughing and partying in the back of the car at the moment of impact. Her reptile brain connected the pain of the accident to the laughter she heard at that moment. Of course, her cortex knew that laughter didn't cause the accident. But large amounts of pain create large cortisol circuits before the cortex can filter and sculpt them. When the girl hears laughter, her cortisol circuit triggers an urgent drive to do something to avoid pain, but she doesn't know what to do.

This quirky sense of danger promotes survival in an amazing way. Imagine a lizard being seized by an eagle. The claws digging into his sides trigger cortisol, which fuses all the neurons active at that moment. That includes everything going on *before* the pain, because electrical activity lasts for a few moments. A precise early-warning detector is thus built effortlessly. The smell of an eagle as it swoops in and the sudden darkness caused by an eagle blocking out the sun are now linked to the lizard's cortisol. If he manages to free himself and survive, he will have a very effective new circuit. Thus, cortisol circuits enable a reptile to avoid death without actually "knowing" what death is, or even what an eagle is.

The Memory of Pain Has a Purpose

Pain wires us with warning signs. When it's big pain, we may build big warning circuits that get labeled phobias or posttraumatic stress. Smaller pain builds smaller warning circuits that we're less aware of. We end up with alarmed feelings that don't always make sense. It would be nice if we could just delete a circuit that made bad predictions. But there's a good survival reason why we can't. Imagine your ancestor watching someone die from eating a poison berry. His cortisol would surge and he would remember that berry forever. Years later, on a day when he was very hungry, he would be able to resist eating that berry. Your ancestor survived because his cortisol circuits endured.

Today's "Survival" vs. Our Ancestors'

Your cortisol circuits endure and create life-or-death feelings that are hard to make sense of. You know you won't actually die if you fail to get that hoped-for promotion, or if someone pulls your hair on the playground. You know you won't die if there's a long line at the post office and you end up getting a parking ticket. But your neurochemicals evolved to give you a sense of life-threatening urgency when you face a setback.

Modern life is often blamed for this feeling, though our ancestors lived with harsher survival challenges. If you had lived in the past, vermin would have infested your home, your food, and your drinking water. You would have felt sores irritating your skin most of the time. You would have watched siblings die. Your neighbors would invade, rape, and pillage. You would not have been free to choose your sex partner. Cortisol would have given you that "do something" feeling often, and you wouldn't always have had a way to make it stop.

Cortisol creates the belief that life is worse today. When you worry about the SATs or looking fat, cortisol creates the physical sense of imminent annihilation. When you think about threats your ancestors faced, no cortisol doom is triggered because direct experience is what builds cortisol circuits, and you share little direct experience with your ancestors.

People who tell you life is awful these days are trying to validate your threatened feelings to win your support. You may find it hard to believe your threatened feelings could be caused by mere small annoyances. You keep scanning for evidence of bigger threats, and many people will offer you such evidence. If you watch the news or listen to political speeches, you will feel sure that the world is on the verge of collapse. The world does not collapse, but you don't celebrate because they immediately capture your attention with a new sign of cataclysm. It leaves you feeling worse, but you're afraid to stop watching because that leaves you alone with your threatened feelings.

Generational Differences

We like to challenge the fears of our elders, of course. You probably imagine your ancestor heroically eating that berry and proving it was harmless all along. Life would be easy if old warnings were always false, and your friends' warnings were always true. The world is more complex, alas, and a person who ignored poison-berry warnings whenever he got hungry would have died and his genes would be gone. Our genes come from people who held on to their stored experience. This mechanism may seem flawed, but it's much more efficient than being hard-wired for dangers at birth. We learn from experience instead of being born to fear whatever threatened our ancestors. Each generation of humans can learn about danger from its own cortisol surges. We learn about danger from our elders as well, but each generation tends to sneer at the fears of its elders and build fears of its own.

I learned this in a painful way. My mother once told me she was up all night fearing the milk would spoil because she forgot it on the counter. I sneered at her anxiety. But after she died, I realized that when she was a child, she would have gone hungry if she left the milk out. Her three sisters would have gone hungry too, because she was responsible for feeding them when she was only a child herself. Real pain built connections in her brain that were always there.

I wish I had understood this when she was alive. The best I can do is celebrate my brain's ability to learn from my own experience. Her fears were part of my experience thanks to mirror neurons. I didn't have to learn by playing in traffic and eating poison berries, thanks to her fears. I built my own threat detector, and it may have quirks of its own.

Extrapolating from Experiences

The human brain generalizes from past pain. Sometimes we overreact, but we'd be worse off if we didn't learn from pain. Jellyfish don't generalize the way humans do, so if they burn one tentacle on a hot stove, the other tentacles will still touch it. Your brain is a central clearing-house that links past pain to potential future pain. We anticipate threats so efficiently that we agonize over statistical projections that 1 person per 10 million will be harmed twenty years from now. We feel threatened when the boss lifts one eyebrow by a millimeter. It's hard to be so good at anticipating pain.

EXERCISE: YOUR PERSONAL SECURITY ALARM

Whatever triggered cortisol in your past built neural pathways that alert you to avoid harm today. You can call it stress, anxiety, fear, or panic depending on the intensity, but cortisol makes you feel like something awful will happen if you don't do something now. It's hard to know what turns it on because it's just electricity flowing down a well-developed chain of neurons. But if you pay careful attention to your bad feelings, you can find patterns. That helps you make new decisions about avoiding harm instead of just flowing with old information. Bad feelings may still come because the pathways are still there. But when you know it's an old response to an old threat, you stop seeking evidence to feed it, so the feeling just passes. Explore your threatened feelings and find examples of:

A threatened feeling that fits the pattern of your adolescent threats

_____

_____

_____

A threatened feeling that fits the pattern of your early childhood threats

_____

_____

_____

A threatened feeling that fits the pattern of a parent's sense of threat

_____

_____

_____

A threatened feeling that fits the pattern of threats that bond your social circle

_____

_____

_____

Social Pain and the Mammal Brain

Mammals alleviate the feeling of imminent threat by congregating in groups. Herds make it easier to relax while remaining alert for danger. Herd behavior has a bad ring to it today, but the math proves that safety in numbers promotes survival better than the every-reptile-for-himself lifestyle. Mammals have a higher life expectancy than most earlier species, and their babies have higher survival rates too. But all is not warm and fuzzy in the mammal world. Social groups trigger bad feelings as well as good feelings. When the brain adapted to group life, a new kind of unhappiness evolved: social pain.

Social isolation is a survival threat in the state of nature. Natural selection created social pain to warn you of a threat to your social bonds the same way that physical pain warns you of a threat to your body. When you see images of herd animals, you may think they are enjoying a nice sense of solidarity. But if you look close, you find that each individual brain struggles to find a safe place.

Imagine you're a wildebeest seeking greener pastures with your herd. When you reach a river, you fear pain from a crocodile if you jump in alone, so you stop to watch what others do. While you're analyzing this, the herd builds up behind you and you fear they'll push you in. That would be even more dangerous, so you decide to do something fast. When you jump, others quickly jump with you because crocodiles eat stragglers. You feel pain from hooves and horns tumbling around you.

These social complications are not obvious when you see a video of wildebeest leaping majestically into a river. It looks like they fit in effortlessly. We humans value our individuality and don't just follow the crowd. But when you move away from a group, huge cortisol spikes often take you by surprise. Your brain is inherited from creatures that monitored their group mates to survive. Critters indifferent to the group got weeded out of the gene pool, and a brain that monitors social dynamics was selected for.

Animals with bigger brains have bigger social ups and downs. Small-brained mammals tend to size each other up once and build a lasting circuit. Primates have enough neurons to keep updating their feelings about each other.

What Are Mirror Neurons?

Primates have special neurons that facilitate social bonds. These mirror neurons activate when an individual watches the behavior of others. Scientists discovered mirror neurons by accident. They were studying the electrical activity in a monkey's brain while it grasped a peanut. When the experiment was over, a researcher picked up the peanut to put it away. To his amazement, the monkey's brain lit up with the same electrical pattern observed when it picked up the peanut itself. Watching an action stimulates the same neural trail as executing the action.

We do not mirror everything we see in others. Mirror neurons only fire when you watch someone get a reward or face a threat. The firing is much weaker than executing an action yourself. But if you repeatedly watch another person get a reward or face a threat, connections build. You wire yourself to get the reward or avoid the threat in the way that you've seen. This research is in its infancy, but it has been learned that songbirds have mirror neurons, and they learn their songs by listening to others.

The Added Dimension of Empathy

Mirror neurons allow us to feel other people's pain. This has a benefit, as often suggested by empathy researchers, but it also has a cost. You can get wired to suffer just by being around people who suffer. Even if your life is fine, mirroring builds a pathway to your cortisol. Once your physical sense of threat is turned on, your cortex looks for evidence of threat. It will find evidence because that eases the "do something" feeling.

Social groups build a shared sense of threat. When your social group feels threatened, you notice. You are free to dismiss the alarm in your own mind. But your group mates may expect you to empathize with their pain pattern. If you don't, your social bonds may be threatened. Your group mates may decide you are not "one of us." They may even see *you* as the threat. It's not easy being a primate.

Groups vs. Individuality

We all face a constant choice between striking out alone and doing what it takes to stick with a group. You don't consciously believe you will die without social support, but the neurochemical response to this prospect is surprisingly strong. For example, if your work is criticized at a performance review, you know your survival is not literally threatened, but cortisol makes it feel that way. The alarm tells your cortex to search for threats, and your cortex cooperates by finding some.

NATURE'S OUTCASTS
Animals sometimes eject an individual from the group. The most common examples are deposed alphas and adolescent males. Cortisol spikes in an ostracized animal, and indeed they often perish. Animals fear exclusion so intensely that they typically do what it takes to stay with the group, even when dominated harshly. A mammal will leave the group when it promotes reproduction because the big cortisol surge is offset by a big happy-chemicals surge.

Becoming Independent

Social pain is an inevitable part of growing up. You start out with a degree of social support, but at some point you learn that your parents cannot protect you forever. This is poignantly clear among monkeys marked as juveniles by a tuft of white fur. The troop cuts you slack until the white fur is gone at three months of age. Then you're fair game and adult monkeys will snatch food from your mouth. It may feel like something is wrong with the world when childhood ends and you face threats for yourself. Yet this is the way of nature. No species could survive unless its young learned survival skills before its parents died. Cortisol surges when you face threats without the protection of your elders. So every brain wires itself with the pain of losing social support.

The Benefits of Social Pain

This social pain circuit is a useful tool. It helps you choose between social rewards and other rewards. Imagine you're offered a great promotion in another state. You feel bad at the thought of losing the life you have, but the idea of passing up the career advancement feels bad too. Bad feelings help the brain weigh one risk against others. Cortisol helps you interpret information, even when you have two good choices. Daily life is filled with choices between the bad feeling of lost opportunity when you stick with the herd and the bad feeling of being isolated and ignored. These bad feelings do not mean the world is bad. They are just a tool.

Today's Focus on Social Pain

Social pain is not new to the world, but your brain gives it less attention when you're experiencing hunger, violence, hard labor, and disease. Once you're free from physical pain, as many of us are on a daily basis, social pain grabs your attention. Every possible threat to your social bonds looms large. Anything resembling the social pain of your past will light up your well-paved pathway and turn on your cortisol. Warning signs are wired in, so the slightest hint of that old familiar pain can quickly trigger a big surge.

You have power over which information you focus on. But the choice is not simple. On the one hand, you want to avoid false alarms. On the other hand, you want to respect the alarm calls of your herd mates to avoid losing that social support. To make matters worse, just belonging to the herd doesn't make your mammal brain happy. It wants to be noticed.

Why Your Brain Equates Attention with Survival

Exclusion makes you unhappy, but inclusion does not necessarily make you happy. Once you're in a group, you see others getting what you are not getting. You feel bad, though you hate to admit it. There's a good physical reason for this pervasive source of unhappiness. The first experience in your brain, the circuit at the foundation of your neural network, is the sense that you will die if you don't get attention.

It Starts Early

The fragility of a newborn human is unparalleled in nature. No other creature is born so far from being able to survive on his own. Consider:

- A gazelle can run with the herd the day after it's born.
- An elephant can walk before its first meal, since that's how it gets to the nipple.
- A fish is an orphan from birth because its parents swim off once the eggs are fertilized.
- Yet a human cannot even lift his head for weeks, and he can't provide for himself and his offspring for decades.

We humans are born with an unfinished nervous system for a good reason. If we developed fully *in utero*, our heads would be too big to fit through the birth canal. Instead, we get born premature, with a nervous system that isn't hooked up. This was learned by comparing human infants to premature chimpanzees. A premature chimp is not capable of holding on to its mother as she swings through the trees the way a full-term baby chimp can. A newborn human is like a premature chimp with a much bigger brain. Our brains kept growing bigger as our ancestors succeeded at getting more protein and fat. They thrived on bone marrow from scavenged bones even before they excelled at hunting. Bigger brains led to better hunting methods, more nutrition, and even bigger brains. So our species got born at ever earlier stages of development, with a lot of neurons, but fewer connections between them.

A chimpanzee is born with eyes and limbs that are ready to go. Humans link up their sensory organs and musculoskeletal system after birth, from direct experience. When a newborn human sees a hand flying in front of her face, she does not know she's attached to that hand, no less that she can control it. We are born helpless and we hook up our brains gradually during a long period of dependency. This gives us the advantage of adapting our nervous system to the environment we're born into, but it also means we start life with an extreme sense of vulnerability.

Fortunately, the vulnerability of the human baby sparked communication. A baby that could call attention to its needs was more likely to survive. Mothers good at interpreting their babies' signals had more surviving DNA. Thus, the ability to communicate was naturally selected for. When we succeed, our needs are met and happy chemicals flow. When we fail, cortisol flows and we look for a way to do something. Eventually, we develop complex communication circuits, but they rest on the core sense that you will die if you are not heard. You don't think this in words, but you think it with neurochemicals.

When you were born, you experienced pain that you couldn't do anything about. The resulting cortisol made you cry. That worked! It got your needs met. A newborn doesn't cry as a conscious act of communication. It doesn't cry because it knows what milk is. It cries because that's one of our few prewired circuits. A baby soon learns to stop crying because it recognizes signs of relief from its past. It stops crying before its needs are actually met because it has linked attention to relief.

But a baby learns that attention can vanish as quickly as it came. Social support disappears for reasons a baby doesn't understand. When a baby feels safe, it ventures out to explore, and pain strikes again in some unexpected way. We must explore beyond the cocoon of social support to wire up our brains, so we experience threat and learn to manage it. No amount of nurturing can protect us from the reality of human vulnerability.

Your Early Circuits Remain with You Today

Your early vulnerability circuits are still there. When your poetry is ignored by the one you love, or your views are ignored at a meeting, these circuits send electricity to your cortisol. We don't consciously think it's a matter of life and death to be seen and heard, but old circuits make it feel that way.

The bad feeling of being ignored is compounded when you see others getting attention. In every troop of primates, some individuals get more attention than others. Field researchers have documented the way baboons give their attention to some troop mates more than others. Laboratory researchers find that chimpanzees will exchange food for a chance to look at photos of the alpha chimp in their group. Your brain seeks attention as if your life depended on it because in the state of nature, it does. When the expectation is disappointed, cortisol flows.

EXERCISE: MAKE IT STOP

It's hard to stop your cortisol because your brain is designed to protect you from threats. Your ancestors conquered hunger, cold, and predators because cortisol made them feel bad until they found a way to make it stop. Once your physical needs are met, social threats get your attention. That's why you feel like your survival is threatened when anything reminds you of social frustrations you experienced in youth. It's hard to "do something" about this cortisol because the source of the threat is not clear. It helps to focus your attention elsewhere, which is why we develop habits that distract us from cortisol. Some of these "happy habits" are good for you in the long run, and others are not. Pulling your hair out when you feel bad is not sustainable, but weaving a basket is. Hopping on a plane to Vegas is not sustainable in the long run, but chatting with your Aunt Millie is. Notice the habits you use to shift out of distressing thoughts. Consider the consequences of each habit, and decide whether it serves your long-term well-being:

Cortisol-stopping habits that hurt me in the long run

_____

_____

_____

Cortisol-stopping habits that serve me in the long run

_____

_____

_____

The Unquenchable Thirst for Status

Most people find it hard to believe that their cortisol is caused by status concerns. It's easy to say "I don't care about status," though you can easily see that others care. You may not care about one particular status marker, like the latest gadget or clothing brand. But your mammal brain is always comparing you to others and deciding who's on top. When it's the other guy, your cortisol is released. In the state of nature, that would warn you to hold back and avoid harmful conflict. Today, you get a vague feeling that you're threatened by anyone you see in the one-up position. You don't think that consciously, but your mammal brain wants to avoid the one-down position as if your life depended on it. And thus it drives you to seek the one-up position, though you'd never consider yourself a one-upper.

These nagging impulses are hard to make sense of because you don't think this in words. Many people make peace with their mammal brain by deciding that the world is forcing this on them. But it doesn't work. Your one-down feelings are intensified when you feel judged by the world. You are better off knowing that you are participating in the judging. When you know you are creating the "do something" feeling yourself, you have power over it.

Status in the Animal World

It helps to know how animals one-up each other. One simple example is the quest to look bigger. Mammals stand their hair on end without conscious intent because cortisol tightens hair follicles. (That's the equivalent of human goose bumps.) When your hair stands out, adversaries think you're bigger than you are. Bigger animals seize food, mates, and even babies from smaller group mates, so looking big promotes survival. Bad feelings make it happen. (Oft-repeated disclaimer: I'm not saying you should do this; I'm saying you have more power over your impulses when you understand them.)

Animal status-consciousness is easy to understand when you know how it happens. When a cow reaches puberty or joins a new herd, she fights each other cow once. If she loses, she associates that cow's smell with pain. If she wins, she feels safe around that cow. Her brain links each herd mate to either her cortisol or her serotonin. That guides her social interactions, as she either submits to avoid pain or dominates to meet her needs. A herd is typically led by an "alpha" cow, who is the unchallenged queen for life. When she dies, the more dominant cows will challenge each other for her spot. Then things go back to normal. Cows don't have enough neural plasticity to keep updating their circuits.

Primates do, however. While small-brained mammals typically keep one status ranking for life, big-brained primates challenge the status hierarchy when they think they can win. Monkeys and apes quickly notice when a troop mate shows weakness, and they challenge them over food, mates, or just who gets the good seat. That doesn't mean they fight all the time—they still avoid fighting when they anticipate pain. They use their big brains to build social alliances that threaten rivals with pain. Research shows that each primate in a group is aware of its own status in relation to each other troop mate, and the relative status of any two third parties. When conflict changes those rankings, each brain rewires itself to reflect the new status hierarchy. The rewards for status are often quite small, but they get the brain's attention when it's not busy meeting a more urgent need. Brains good at status-seeking made more copies of themselves, and the rest is history.

Animals care intensely about the status of their mating partners. Each species has its own strategies for judging potential mates, and they always focus on traits that are uncannily relevant to the survival potential of offspring. For example:

- Peacocks with more colorful tails actually have higher resistance to deadly parasites, which gives their offspring a survival edge.

- In the chimpanzee world, status-seeking tends to trump courtship. That's because males are only interested in fertile females, which means a five-year wait on average, because females are infertile while lactating. Males spend that time jockeying for position against each other.

You may say you don't care about status, but when a high-status person notices you, your happy chemicals soar. Raising your children's status thrills your mammal brain even more. When your specialness is overlooked, your unhappy chemicals spike, and if your children's specialness is overlooked, it's much worse.

Status in Today's World

You may blame these ups and downs on "our society" without recognizing the universality of these impulses. If every mammal in the room has eyes for the same beauty, we end up with many unhappy mammals. If all parents want their children to get into the same high-status institution, a lot of cortisol will flow. If everyone wants to be chief, unhappiness will reign. Such impulses are found in every culture and in our animal ancestors, so it's futile to blame "our culture."

Your feelings about your status are independent of your socioeconomic circumstances. Imagine you're a high-priced lawyer with a lot of formal status trappings. Every minute of your waking life is spent kowtowing to clients and senior partners and anyone who can help your career. Everywhere you look, you see threats that could destroy your career. You do not feel dominant. You might actually be happier if you were a bus driver who rules the bus all day and then rules the roost at home. Status does not come from fixed labels and abstract words. It's the feeling you get when you interact with others. Those feelings change from moment to moment as we go through our day, but they depend heavily on the circuits we've already built.

We tell ourselves that status doesn't matter and everyone is equal, but each brain keeps monitoring how it stacks up against others. Expectations build from experience. When your expectations are exceeded, happy chemicals flow. When your expectations are disappointed, it feels like a survival threat, even if you consciously know better. Everyone is sensitive to slights because everyone wants to be special. The urge for specialness might seem annoying in others, but in yourself, it just feels like fairness.

EXERCISE: THE URGE TO BE SPECIAL

Being special promotes survival in the state of nature. Your mammal brain seeks specialness as if your life depended on it. Whatever made you feel special when you were young triggered happy chemicals that connected neurons. These connections trigger expectations about how to survive. When your expectations about specialness are disappointed, it feels like a survival threat. It's easy to see this in others, but hard to see in yourself. We imagine ourselves having "good reasons" for our motivations, but a quest for specialness does not sound like a "good reason." This leaves us confused about the reasons for our neurochemical ups and downs. Small social disappointments can give you the feeling of grave danger without knowing why. These surges have less power if you know where they come from. Make a habit of noticing the urge to be special, in yourself and in others. Instead of denying this urge, notice your expectations and the unhappiness you feel when your expectations are disappointed. Although it's tempting to condemn yourself for these feelings, you can honor the mammalian energy that kept your ancestors alive. Notice examples of:

The urge to be special in others

_____

_____

The urge to be special in yourself

_____

_____

The urge to be special in your ancestors

_____

_____

Disappointments in the quest for specialness

_____

_____

Your brain compares itself to others even if you wish it didn't. In the state of nature, comparing yourself to others promotes survival. It protects you from getting into fights that you are likely to lose. When your brain sees you are weaker than another individual, it releases cortisol to remind you of the risk. This helps you hold back, despite your urge to promote your survival interests. Unhappy chemicals help us inhibit our urge for dominance and thus get along with group mates. We need unhappy chemicals, as much as we'd rather live without them.

The Cortex's Role in Threat-Seeking

The human cortex creates abstractions that feel real. We can terrorize ourselves with our own thoughts because of our ability to activate circuits internally instead of just relying on inputs reaching the senses. For example, you can begin to sweat just thinking about an upcoming work presentation, even though you're not actually in the room, ready to begin talking. This allows us to imagine future threats and take action to avoid them. We can even imagine our own mortality: We know something will kill us, even though we don't know what. This motivates us to keep seeking potential threats instead of just waiting for our senses to report what's there.

The Chemical Roller Coaster of Threats

Identifying a potential threat feels curiously good. You're like a gazelle that smells a lion and can't relax until it sees where the lion is. Seeing a lion feels good when the alternative is worse. We seek evidence of threats to feel safe, and we get a dopamine boost when we find what we seek. You can also get a serotonin boost from the feeling of being right, and an oxytocin boost from bonding with those who sense the same threat. This is why people seem oddly pleased to find evidence of doom and gloom. But the pleasure doesn't last because the "do something" feeling commands your attention again. You can end up feeling bad a lot even if you're successful in your survival efforts.

A Big Cortex Has a Big Threat Response

A small cortex scans for threats it has actually experienced, but a big cortex like a human's can build chains of associations from bits and parts of actual experience. You can think about a future that you can't smell or touch. You can imagine disaster scenarios quite distant from your physical reality. And you can imagine what the world will be when you are gone. Knowing the world will go on without you someday is more distressing than we realize. It's so upsetting that you're tempted to imagine the world ending when you end. Then you won't be missing anything.

I noticed this conundrum at a lecture on future energy reserves. When the speaker presented a chart projecting world energy reserves a hundred years from now, everyone in the audience had to imagine a world they would not be part of. The threat of collapse found a receptive audience—indeed, it was almost a relief, because the thought of living at the important time in history feels better than the thought of being gone without a trace. Feeling important helps relieve distress, even when we imagine we are only interested in facts. The cortex looks for facts that make you feel good.

Your cortex promotes survival by looking for logical explanations of what your mammal brain feels is true. If you feel that things are falling apart, for example, you will find evidence that things are falling apart and overlook evidence of things going well. A big cortex attached to a mammal brain can easily conclude that the world is going to hell in a handbasket. (More on this in my book *Beyond Cynical: Transcend Your Mammalian Negativity*.)

You may feel sure that you're focused on facts and couldn't possibly be so biased. But your brain actually has ten times more neurons telling your eyes what to look for than it has to take things in randomly. That is, ten times more neurons send information from the cortex to the eyes than from the eyes to the cortex. We are designed to scan for inputs we've already experienced as important rather than wasting our attention on whatever comes along.

It helps to know how the cortex finds facts that fit expectations. A clear example is the way your cortex reads this page. It does not just take in details passively. It generates expectations about the chunk of detail that will come next, based on past experience. Dopamine is released when you see a chunk that matches your expectations. You extract meaning and move on to generate an expectation about the next chunk. If a chunk fails to match your expectations, cortisol is released, which prompts you to take a closer look before you create meaning and move on. You're not conscious of generating expectations before you read a word, but you'd never be able to read if you didn't.

Expectations vs. Reality

Your expectations are neural pathways that light up in anticipation of sensory inputs. This makes a smooth flow of meaning possible. Which expectations you activate depend on your stock of life experience and the neurochemicals you are experiencing at the moment.

Your cortex is always making predictions about future pain and future rewards. But anticipated rewards don't always materialize, which is another source of cortisol. Your cortex can imagine a better world that makes you happy all the time, but you fail to find this utopia. Reality is often a disappointment, and it's hard to understand the role of your expectations because your cortex generates them so effortlessly.

A lizard never thinks something is wrong with the world, even as it watches its young get eaten alive. It doesn't tell itself "something is wrong with the world," because it doesn't have enough neurons to imagine the world being other than what it is. It doesn't expect a world in which there are no predators, so it doesn't condemn the world for falling short of expectations. It doesn't condemn itself for failing to keep its offspring alive. Humans expect more, and we do something about it. That's why we end up focused on our disappointments instead of saluting our accomplishments.

EXERCISE: WHAT ARE YOUR EXPECTATIONS?

Life feels good when it exceeds your expectations, and bad when it falls short of your expectations. Your ups and downs depend heavily on your expectations, so it's important to understand them. Expectations are neural pathways that you electrically activate in anticipation of incoming information. You activate them without conscious intent because your electricity flows where it has flowed before. Your brain is always comparing the neurons activated by your senses to the neurons you've preactivated. When it finds a pattern that matches, you "know" what you are experiencing and whether it is good or bad for you. Your emotions are easier to make sense of when you learn to notice your expectations. Notice examples of:

A time you expected harm and ended up feeling harmed

_____

_____

_____

_____

_____

A time you expected rewards and ended up feeling rewarded

_____

_____

_____

_____

_____

Once you do this with big expectations, start noticing the smaller expectations you generate many times an hour.

When a monkey loses a banana to a rival, he feels bad, but he doesn't expand the problem by thinking about it over and over. He looks for another banana. He ends up feeling rewarded rather than harmed. Humans use their extra neurons to construct theories about bananas and end up constructing pain. For example, imagine that a bully steals your parking spot once a year. By the time you are thirty-six years old, your brain has stored twenty chunks of evidence that the world is full of bullies. This template in your brain can divert your electricity from the abundant evidence of people being good to you. To complicate matters further, you may have misperceived those parking lot incidents in the first place. Haven't you ever been accused of taking someone's spot when you are sure you were there first? It's easy to misjudge a situation when your eyes are busy driving. Yet it's hard to notice your own misjudgments because electricity flows so easily along your well-worn pathways. A brain can construct an image of a bad world despite abundant evidence of good.

Accepting the Value in Unhappiness

When a pattern-seeking human cortex is hooked up to a dominance-seeking mammal brain and a danger-avoiding reptile brain, it's not surprising that we end up with a lot of cortisol alarms. It's useful to remember that cortisol prevents pain as well as causing it.

For example, lizards run from me the moment I step outside my door. Most of this alarmism is for nothing, because I do not step on lizards. But reptiles don't fault themselves for excessive caution. False positives are part of the reptilian survival system.

We humans hate false positives. We want to duck bullets, but we don't want to duck when there's no bullet. We expect our alarm system to call the shots perfectly every time. I think about this when I watch the meerkats at the zoo. They run for cover when a plane flies overhead, though no plane has ever tried to eat them. Meerkats did not evolve to live in zoos near airports, but they did evolve in places where birds of prey could grab them in an instant. They survived because of their alertness for a particular pattern of cues—in this case, flying predators. I am not saying we should fear everything our ancestors feared. I am simply appreciating the meerkats' self-acceptance. They don't castigate themselves for their timidity after the plane passes. They don't berate each other for those bad calls. They just go back to what they were doing before the plane passed: scanning for threats and opportunities.

Cortisol Helps When You're Cautious and When You're Daring

Excess caution often helps us humans survive. I wash my hands before every meal even though my world is quite sanitary. I look in my rearview mirror every time I change lanes even though no car is there much of the time. A person could wear seat belts her whole life without ever being in an accident. Anticipating threats helps us prevent unhappiness in the long run. But over-reliance on this strategy can leave you with endless hand-washing and mirror-checking habits. Sometimes the best strategy is to approach a potential threat and gather information. Cortisol helps you do that, too. It frees you to try new things and still have an effective warning light when you've gone too far. Accepting the bad feelings cortisol creates sounds harsh, but the alternative is worse. You can end up unhappy about being unhappy. Instead, you can accept your own warning system, though it sometimes overreacts to patterns that resemble past threats.

You Can Change and Adapt

When I wish my cortisol would stop, I think about feral pigs. (These are pigs that have escaped from farms and returned to the wild.) They fascinate me because feral pigs start developing the features of wild boars once they start meeting their own survival needs. Their snouts grow bigger when they use those snouts to root for food. Their fur grows longer when they need it for shelter from the cold. In short: the bad feeling of hunger and cold triggers the strengths the pigs were meant to have. You can trigger the strengths you were meant to have when you understand your threat responses.

4 | THE VICIOUS CYCLE OF HAPPINESS

The Slide from Happiness to Disappointment

Imagine you're receiving a Lifetime Achievement Award from the Institute of Human Magnificence. You hear wild applause as your name is called. It feels great. A few minutes later, however, the ceremony is over and you are back to who you were before it. Why? Because your happy chemicals have been reabsorbed. Though you may enjoy some more when you reminisce, your brain will go back to scanning for potential threats as well. And it will find some: Was my speech well received? What if they hate my next project? Why didn't my friends come to the ceremony? If you expect your award to bring constant happiness, you will be disappointed.

Everyone's happy chemicals droop, which is why everyone looks for ways to stimulate more. That's how our brain is designed to work. Even if you discovered a new planet, the happy-chemical surge would not last. You could look at your planet every day, but you would not feel the full joy of discovering it in every moment. You would want that feeling again, though. You'd try to fulfill that need with the pathways you have, which might motivate you to look for another planet.

But if you found one just like the last, it would not feel as good as the first time. You'd have to find a bigger planet to get that surge. This brain we've inherited saves the happy chemicals for new information. The same old information does not get them going.

I experienced the brain's indifference to old information in a local flower shop. I was thrilled by a fabulous smell when I walked in the door, and decided to buy a bouquet so I could keep enjoying it. After I paid for the bouquet, I took one last deep breath before heading to my car. I was surprised to find that I hardly smelled anything! It was not new information.

WHY EARLY MEMORIES ARE SO POWERFUL

The fading of happy chemicals motivates us to keep renewing our survival efforts, but it leaves us curiously vulnerable to frustration. You might blame your frustration on "our society" until you understand its physiology. Your brain is always comparing the world to the early experiences that built your circuits. When you were young, everything was new, so you often experienced things as "the best ever" or "the worst ever." That caused a neurochemical surge big enough to wire in a circuit. But the next time you eat the same pizza, it's not "the best you ever had." The next time you suffer the same public humiliation, it's not "the worst you've ever had." Life often falls short of your expectations because you built those expectations when the information was new.

I feel a surge of joy when I smell coffee beans grinding. But if I comment on the smell to the baristas, I've often found that they don't know what I'm talking about. If I got a job at a coffee shop with the expectation of feeling joy all the time, I would be disappointed.

Each of the happy chemicals disappoints in its own way. This chapter explores dopamine disappointment, oxytocin disappointment, endorphin disappointment, and serotonin disappointment. Then we will examine the vicious cycle that results when we rush to relieve bad feelings by stimulating good feelings. You can build a virtuous cycle instead when you understand these impulses.

Dopamine Disappointment

Dopamine is triggered by new rewards. That's why the first lick of an ice cream cone is heaven. Ten licks later, your attention wanders. You start thinking about the next thing on your agenda, and the next. You still love the ice cream, but you don't feel it as much because your brain doesn't see it as new information. Your brain is already looking for the next great way to meet your needs. Old rewards, even creamy, delicious ones, don't command your brain's attention. Scientists call this *habituation*.

The Joy in the New

How can a person be happy with a brain that habituates to good things? Philosophers have long contemplated this dilemma, and now scientists and even gastronomists are getting into the act. The top-rated restaurant in America is based on the science of pleasure. The French Laundry serves only small plates because, according to founder and head chef Thomas Keller, a dish only pleases the palate for the first three or four bites. After that, you are just filling up instead of experiencing ecstasy. So the famous California wine-country establishment triggers joy over and over by sending a lot of tiny new dishes to your table.

What if you went to the French Laundry and fell in love with one particular dish? Imagine that you persuaded the chef to make you a full plate of it. When it comes, you dive in with excitement. But after a few bites, you're disappointed. You wonder if they messed up. Maybe they did something different? No, it's just not new information anymore, so your happy chemicals don't respond. It's hard to believe you're perceiving it differently, because you are not aware of your own habituation.

The brain triggers joy when it encounters any new way to meet its needs. New food. New love. New places. New techniques. After a while, the new thing doesn't measure up. "It's not the way I remember it." You may wish you could trade it in for another new thing. But when you understand your brain, you realize the disappointment comes from you rather than the thing itself.

Dopamine's Role in Survival

Dopamine disappointment is easier to accept when you understand its survival value. Imagine your ancestor finding a river full of fish. He's very excited as he runs back to tell his clan about it. Dopamine creates the energy to run back, and the memory to find the spot again. Then its job is over. Your ancestor might feel happiness in other ways:

- His serotonin might surge when he thinks of the respect he will get for his find.
- His oxytocin might activate when he thinks of the shared pleasure of feasting.

But his dopamine will dip unless he finds an even bigger run of fish. He will look hard for more fish because he knows how good it feels.

Facing a Dopamine Dip

When your dopamine dips, you suddenly notice your cortisol so you're more aware of threats. You want the bad feeling to stop so you look for a way to "do something." You know from experience that an immediate happy-chemical stimulator will work, if only for a moment. This conundrum is easy to imagine from the perspective of a teenager at a gambling casino. He wins $50, and a huge dopamine surge wires his brain to expect a good feeling from gambling. The next time he feels bad, the idea of gambling pops into his head. But when he goes, the great feeling doesn't happen. He keeps expecting it, though, so he keeps gambling. Soon he's feeling bad about all the money he lost. The bad feeling drives him to look for a way to feel better, which activates the thought of more gambling. You can have a gambling habit at any age, but a young brain more easily builds neural highways big enough to outlast multiple disappointments.

Healthy behaviors lead to a dopamine dip as well. Imagine a child winning a spelling bee. She suddenly feels more respect (serotonin) and acceptance (oxytocin) than ever. She wants that good feeling again, so she spends a lot of time studying spelling words. Her dopamine is stimulated each time she mentally seeks and finds the spelling of a word, because she linked that to a big reward. The steady stream of dopamine distracts her from any bad feelings she may have. In a world full of threats you can't control, it's nice to know you can feel good whenever you want just by picking up a dictionary. But the day will come when the habit disappoints. If the girl wins a few more spelling competitions, the thrill will eventually droop. To get more of it, she will set her sights on a new reward. Whether it's the school talent show or getting into medical school, each step will trigger dopamine once she links it to meeting her needs.

Dopamine disappoints whether you've linked it to a healthy or unhealthy way of meeting your needs. Like the juiced-up monkeys in Chapter 2, your brain takes the juice you have for granted instead of cranking out more happy chemicals. But if you lose the juice you took for granted, you're darned unhappy. Managing such a brain is not easy, but it's the responsibility that comes with the gift of life.

The Constant Search for the "First High"

Drug addicts say they are always "chasing the first high." The first use of a drug triggers more pleasure than you could ever get from a natural source of happy chemicals. But the second time, it's no longer the most intense experience ever—unless you take more than you did the first time. You constantly choose between disappointment and taking more.

Our brain chases the first high, whether it's a natural high or an artificial high. Artificial highs build artificially big circuits and have big side effects, but even natural happiness stimulators have harmful side effects if repeated too often. People are tempted to repeat a happy habit despite the consequences because a droop in your happy chemicals leaves you face to face with your cortisol. Whether you are seeking the next margarita or the next career opportunity, your dopamine flows the moment you start seeking it, but when you get it, it's not as thrilling as you expected.

The Thrill of the Chase

The act of seeking is more rewarding than you probably realize. If you decide that a doughnut is the way to feel good, your dopamine flows as you search for a parking spot near the doughnut shop. It's the same mental activity as foraging: scanning the world for details leading to a reward. When you find a parking spot, your dopamine soars. But when you finally get the doughnut, dopamine droops quickly because it has already done its job.

Computer games are alluring because of this urge to seek. But disappointment quickly sets in if you seek the same reward over and over. That's why computer games focus on getting to the next level. You feel excited because you are approaching a new reward, even though it doesn't meet any real needs.

Museums and shopping malls are other popular ways to stimulate the pleasure of seeking. They would lose their appeal if they always looked the same, so new exhibits and new merchandise are always brought in. If you have ever lost interest in a shopping mall or museum or computer game, you might have said "it's not as good as it used to be." You didn't realize the change was in you—you stopped releasing dopamine because there was no new information for your brain to process.

Collecting is a popular hobby because it overcomes dopamine disappointment. A collector always has something to seek. When he finds it, he avoids dopamine droop by starting the next quest.

A collection gives you many "needs" to fill, and you have to process a lot of detail so your mind is always distracted from unhappy chemicals. You can also bond with other collectors to stimulate oxytocin. And if you one-up other collectors, you enjoy serotonin. You never hear collectors say, "I don't need anything else. I'll just enjoy my collection as it is." You have to keep seeking to keep stimulating dopamine.

Planning a project triggers dopamine. A big project like a party, home remodel, or life transition stimulates excitement with each step because you've linked that goal to your needs. Dopamine gets you through the inevitable frustration of a long-term project. But once the party is over or the house is remodeled, your dopamine droops. You don't know why you feel bad, and you think maybe something is wrong. If you start a new project, you feel better.

Travel is a great dopamine stimulator. It bombards your senses with new inputs that you have to process in order to reach your goal of being a worldly person, or just to do a simple task like get breakfast. Planning a trip stimulates dopamine as you anticipate the great feeling of being at your destination. And when you arrive at that tropical paradise with its perfect bands of blue and white, you get a rush of excitement. But in a few minutes, you are busy looking for your toothbrush. The next morning, you may feel excitement again when you wake up and see where you are. But as the day wears on, you become who you were before the vacation.

Dopamine has fueled human accomplishment. Thomas Edison stayed up late, seeking filament for a light bulb. Diseases were cured because researchers spent long hours sifting and sorting details in search of patterns. When they found what they were looking for, they typically set out in search of a new goal. Our brains were not designed for sitting around contemplating what we already have. They don't release excitement for nothing. They were meant to dip after a spurt so we have to do something again.

Romantic love is perhaps the most familiar example of dopamine disappointment. When people are "in love," they don't realize they are riding high on the dopamine of a long quest. But the same old reward does not excite dopamine forever. It dips, and then unhappy chemicals get your attention. You may blame the bad feeling on your partner. You may think your partner is "not who she used to be." You may even decide that a new partner would make you happy, because the last new partner triggered a surge that built a pathway. But if you seek the excitement of new love all the time, you may create a vicious cycle.

EXERCISE: WHEN DOES YOUR DOPAMINE DROOP?

If you bite into a brownie that's the best you ever tasted, the second bite cannot be "the best you've ever tasted." The first bite triggers a surge of dopamine, but the surge fades even as you polish off the brownie. Your brain saves dopamine for new information instead of wasting it on the same old rewards. The same is true when you get a smile from a special someone, or a nice career boost. Your dopamine surges at first, but continued rewards don't trigger continued dopamine. When your dopamine droops, it feels like something is wrong with the world, or with you. That disappointment feels less threatening when you know your brain is making way for the new. Notice your dopamine droop when:

Something doesn't thrill you the way it once did

_____

_____

_____

Something doesn't feel as good as you expected after you get it

_____

_____

_____

Something new excites you after you reach a long-sought goal

_____

_____

_____

Endorphin Disappointment

The great feeling of endorphin always droops in a short time because that promotes survival. Masking pain feels good, but you need to feel your pain in order to take action to relieve it. If you expect constant happiness from endorphin, you will be disappointed.

Exercise triggers the euphoric feeling, but if you repeat the same exercise routine, you won't feel the same response you did the first time. It takes an increase in exertion to the point of pain to stimulate endorphin. So if you took the drastic step of inflicting pain on yourself to get a rush of endorphin, it would take more and more pain to trigger the same good feeling.

Starving yourself stimulates endorphin, but you have to starve more and more to keep getting that feeling. Starving triggers endorphin because it helped our ancestors forage in lean times. The ability to seek on an empty stomach promotes survival. If you've ever missed a couple of meals, you may have started feeling a little high. The good feeling stopped as soon as you ate something, but you ate anyway because you know that nutrition is necessary for survival.

Self-Inflicted Pain Is Not the Way to Happiness

Hurting your body to enjoy the endorphin is a mistaken path to happiness. It can only lead to a tragic vicious cycle in which you continually need to experience more pain to get the same endorphin rush. This cycle of endorphin disappointment helps us understand why people who hurt themselves seem inclined to hurt themselves more. When the oblivion of endorphin is over, you are suddenly face to face with reality. You may not like your reality, but we are not meant to ignore pain except for a brief emergency window. We are meant to live with the droop.

If you don't exercise, you should. But if you count on the endorphin joy you get at first, you may not continue. Exercise feels good even without endorphin because it fills your blood with oxygen that goes to your head. If you think you need to exercise to the point of an endorphin high, you will end up injured. We did not evolve to inflict pain on ourselves intentionally to get an endorphin high. Pain warns you of an imminent survival threat. In the world before emergency rooms and anesthesia, a bad feeling was incentive enough to avoid pain-inflicting behaviors.

Synthetic Endorphin Highs

Opium derivatives (heroin, oxycodone, morphine, codeine) stimulate endorphin, but they have terrible side effects:

1. They undermine your natural happy-chemical mechanism.
2. They mask any pain you have while using them, resulting in dangerous neglect of personal care.
3. You habituate to them, so you need to use more to get the same effect. Harmful side effects accumulate quickly, leading to more unhappy chemicals, more urge to use, and a downward spiral.

Social pain does not trigger endorphin, but the euphoria of endorphin masks social pain. This is why it allures people to the point of enduring physical pain. Tragically, more pain results from this quest for oblivion.

EXERCISE: WHEN DOES YOUR ENDORPHIN DROOP?

Endorphin evolved for emergencies. The euphoria of endorphin doesn't last because we need to feel pain to make good decisions. If you subject your body to pain just to get the endorphin, your body redefines what counts as an emergency. You have to keep subjecting yourself to more pain if you want to keep getting an endorphin high. When your endorphin droops, you suddenly notice the reality of your circumstances. Your brain is designed to notice reality because that promotes survival. It would be nice to laugh your way to constant endorphin highs, but it's good to know that endorphin droop is natural and you are designed to manage the reality that comes with it. Notice your endorphin droop in these situations:

An exercise session that felt good but then you realized you overdid it

_____

_____

_____

A joke that doesn't make you laugh out loud anymore, even though you still like it

_____

_____

_____

A light-headed feeling that ended with a delayed meal

_____

_____

_____

A pain medication that doesn't help as much as it once did

_____

_____

_____

Oxytocin Disappointment

A good way to understand oxytocin disappointment is to imagine yourself getting a massage. The first few moments feel phenomenal. Then your mind drifts, and you can literally forget that you are receiving a massage. You enjoy it, of course, but the oxytocin explosion doesn't last. You might blame your massage therapist, unless you know that your brain habituates to things, even great things.

Oxytocin is released at birth, easing the stress of coming into the world. But soon you need more. Animals lick their young and humans cuddle them to induce the release of oxytocin. The flow of oxytocin wires the child to trust the parent and to release oxytocin in similar circumstances. It would be nice to enjoy that feeling all the time, but if you think you can love everyone everywhere, you would take candy from strangers and eventually buy bridges from strangers. Your oxytocin must turn off after it turns on so you can respond to new information about your social environment.

Betrayed Trust and the Oxytocin Droop

Oxytocin protected your ancestors from leaving the tribe every time someone got on their nerves. It saved them from the dangers that befall lone individuals in the wilderness. Today, oxytocin protects you from quitting your job the minute a coworker wrinkles his forehead at you. It keeps you from running away from home the minute your relatives cluck their tongues at your latest adventure. When your oxytocin is flowing, it's easier to overlook reminders of past disappointments and betrayals.

But when an oxytocin spurt fades, your past disappointments are suddenly more accessible. You can be so alert for threats that you feel attacked by a slight change in tone. Social threats seem to expand when the bubble of oxytocin is gone.

Children on a playground learn about social trust. When they get support, the good feeling wires them to expect more where that came from. When their cortisol is triggered, they learn not to expect support in certain quarters. If a classmate helps you with homework, you feel good and a path to your oxytocin is paved. But if a trusted companion insists on copying your homework, you have a dilemma.

Unhealthy Alliances and Oxytocin Disappointment

Oxytocin creates the bonds that lead to gangs, wars, battered spouse syndrome, and perjuring yourself to protect allies from the consequences of their actions. People do drastic things to sustain their oxytocin bonds because an oxytocin droop feels like a survival threat.

My grandparents came from Sicily, where the Mafia builds social bonds with the threat of violence. Mafias offer the illusion of safety by promising protection from violence if you cooperate. You're not safe for long, alas, because the predators will see you as prey rather than an ally when it meets their needs. You learn that you cannot trust anyone. This sense of isolation leaves you feeling so endangered that you're eager to trust those who offer protection and goodwill gestures. A vicious oxytocin cycle results.

No one mentioned the Mafia when I was growing up, and I presumed it was an invention of Hollywood. But when I researched my cultural heritage, I was horrified to discover the wretched lives of my ancestors. Surviving in a culture of violence means choosing at every moment between the survival threat of not cooperating and the survival threat of cooperating. Trust sounds like a virtue, but trusting a predator who expects complete submission may not promote survival ... or it may. The uncertainty is staggering.

Gangs are an especially tragic example of oxytocin disappointment, because young brains are involved. Young people join gangs for protection from aggression, yet end up subjected to more aggression. The impulse is easy to understand in animals because common enemies keep a mammal group together despite internal aggression:

- A zebra is often bitten by a herd mate, but it sticks with the herd because a lion quickly eats it if it leaves.
- Monkeys and elephants stick with their groups despite harsh domination because their young are eaten alive if they leave.
- Even lions and wolves stick with their groups because their meals are stolen by rival packs if they go it alone.

Gangs, like herds, stick together despite enormous internal aggression because they fear external aggression even more. A gang needs the aggression of rival gangs to keep up the safe feeling associated with membership. Oxytocin makes it feel good to be "one of the gang" until the next betrayal, and the conflict keeps cycling.

Battered spouse syndrome and battered child syndrome are similar tragedies of oxytocin disappointment. Abused individuals sometimes cover up for their abusers instead of promoting their own survival. They blame themselves for the betrayal of trust and desperately seek ways to rekindle it. Instead of building new trust with new people, they keep trying to build it with the abuser because they're wired to expect good feelings from them.

An alcoholic looking for someone to drink with is another example of oxytocin disappointment. People seek trust from those they expect to give it to them. Eaters bond with eaters, drug users bond with drug users, shoppers bond with shoppers, and angry ragers bond with angry ragers. These bonds help you feel good about yourself despite your drinking or shopping or raging. But when you decide to get control of your habit, you may be shocked to find that these allies do not support you. They may even undermine your efforts to conquer your habit. Many people end up continuing an unhealthy habit rather than risk their friendships. They tell themselves their "friends" make them feel good. The nice, safe feeling of trust doesn't last, of course, so they keep seeking the safety of social alliances in the ways that worked before.

The pain of disappointed trust enters every life. We all seek safety from social bonds and occasionally discover that we are less safe than we thought. That's why it's important to keep updating your information about your social alliances. You may find that you have a lot more choices than you realized. If you try to sustain your oxytocin at any price, you might overlook real threats. Oxytocin disappointment feels bad, but it frees you to make good survival decisions about the world around you.

The Big Happy Family

You may think good parenting could wire a brain for endless oxytocin. Or that you'd enjoy an endless flow if you were accepted by a particular group. It would be nice to have a safe sense of belonging all the time, and it's tempting to dream of a world that makes this happen for you. But reality keeps falling short of this dream because people are mammals.

If your parents put your needs first when you were young, disappointment strikes when you learn that the rest of the world doesn't treat you this way. And if your parents were not worthy of your trust, then you learned about disappointment even earlier. Either way, oxytocin droop is distressing, but it enables young mammals to transfer their attachment from their mother to their peers, and thus to reproduce.

Fitting In

You may have dreamed of joining a group that would make you feel good forever, and then felt disillusioned when you were finally accepted by it. It's easy to idealize people from afar, especially people whose protection you seek. Once you gain admission, you see that these people are, well, mammals. You might start thinking that *another* group or organization would make you happy forever. A vicious cycle can result. Making new pathways to turn on your oxytocin will help break that cycle.

> **KNOWING YOUR GROUP**
>
> Most species have distinctive markings that instantly separate members from nonmembers. An antelope with one black stripe on its butt can instantly distinguish itself from antelopes with two black stripes or one black and one white stripe. This is how it avoids following the wrong crowd into an ecological niche it's not adapted to. Human groups are also known for their distinctive markings, including popular accessories, physical traits, and learned mannerisms.

In-group conflict is inevitable because each group member has a mammal brain that evolved to promote its own genes.

Animals stick with groups that are full of internal conflict because they are so threatened by external conflict. The more threatened you feel by life outside the group, the more pain you tolerate from within it. Each time you distance yourself from the group, your oxytocin falls and reminds you of the threat of isolation.

We are meant to experience oxytocin dips, despite the discomfort. Trust is nice, but too much trust can threaten survival:

- Imagine a child who trusts his parents to tie his shoes and cut his meat for too long.
- Imagine a student who trusts others to do her homework for her.
- Imagine a spouse who trusts his partner to deal with the world for him.

The nice feeling of trust may distract you from building skills you need to promote your own survival. You could lean on others to avoid the bad feeling of your own limitations, but you might end up with more frustration. That would trigger an urge to "do something," which you might respond to by leaning again on others instead of building skills.

EXERCISE: WHEN DOES YOUR OXYTOCIN DROOP?

Oxytocin droops when you get too far from the herd. Whether they've left you behind or you've wandered astray, the droop alerts you to the fact that you lack social support. Suddenly, it feels like you're facing survival threats alone. It would be nice to enjoy the good feeling of social support all the time, but if you stayed with the herd every minute, you'd miss out on other things. We are designed to find the best way to meet our needs instead of just following other people's quest to meet their needs. Losing support is distressing, but we are not meant to enjoy a constant stream of oxytocin. We are meant to balance the urge for social support against our other long-term needs. You can learn to notice your own skill at doing that. Notice examples of:

A time when you felt endangered by a lack of social support

_____

_____

_____

A time when you lost trust in your social support

_____

_____

_____

A time when you strayed from social support to seek other rewards

_____

_____

_____

Serotonin Disappointment

When people respect you, serotonin surges and it wires you to expect more good feelings in similar ways. But after a while, the same old respect doesn't thrill you. You search for a way to get more, using past experience as your guide. Sometimes you fail to get the respect you seek, despite your best efforts.

When other people are trapped in a quest for approval, it's easy to see—especially when it's people you don't like. You see how their quest for status soon leads to an even bigger quest. It's hard to notice your own brain caught in this natural quest.

Animals help us understand the brain's urge for more social status as soon as the last serotonin boost droops. When a monkey asserts herself for a banana, the food is soon digested and she must assert herself again to make enough milk for her children to survive.

The Quest for Social Importance

When you go to a shop or a restaurant, the staff treats you with a deference that you don't get in the rest of life. Most of the time, the people around you are as convinced of their cause as you are of yours. If you count on getting deference from others to feel good, you may end up disappointed.

When you see people angling for the "best" table, you may think they are foolish. After all, you know that seating arrangements are not a matter of survival. But when *you* fail to get a good seat, it seems different. Your mammal brain is always monitoring your social position and reacting. It did not evolve to say, "I'm important enough now. I can just relax." It evolved to keep advancing your prospects. That's why:

- A person who buys the latest status object feels frustrated when others catch up.
- A person who gets her dream job soon focuses on the next dream job.
- A person who wants to save the world sees a world that's ever more desperate for his saving. Making the world look bad helps him feel good about his contribution.
- A person who controls others wants them to comply faster to more arbitrary commands.

The quest for respect can have positive consequences as well as negative ones, and much human achievement has been fueled by it. But however you attain your badge of status, the good feeling soon passes and you long for a bigger badge of status. When your serotonin dips, it may feel like something is wrong with the world. When you get the badge of status you seek, the world looks all right ... for a little while.

You may think you'll be happy forever once your poetry is published in the *New York Times*, but your mind would soon seek the next bit of recognition if it did. The brain learns to feel important in a particular way, and then it looks for more of that feeling. When Marlon Brando wails "I coulda been a contender" in *On the Waterfront*, you believe he'd be happy if he'd won a boxing title. But in all probability, he would have contended for more once he got it. And when you watch *Downton Abbey* or *Game of Thrones*, you may consciously hate the powerful, but your mirror neurons enjoy that sense of power, so you go back for more.

We often hear about Hollywood stars who go into a tailspin when their popularity wanes. I used to be confused by this. "Isn't one megahit enough to make a person happy?" I wondered. Now I understand that the good feeling of a megahit trains the brain to seek that particular way of feeling good. If you end up feeling bad instead, you don't see how you created the disappointment. You can blame the ruthlessness of the industry, the fickleness of the public, and the incompetence of management, without recognizing your brain's habit of seeking serotonin in ways that worked before.

This theme pervades private life as well as the movies. Each person seeks respect from those around them in ways they expect to work. Some people impose their wishes on others just for the pleasure of it. And when the pleasure ebbs, they impose again. If they fail to get that deference from others and face the world without the serotonin boost, they crash and burn.

Rescuing others is a popular way to seek respect. Making yourself a hero is a relatively reliable way to feel important, and it helps you avoid conflicts that would erode respect. But the good feeling soon passes and you have to rescue again. Rescuers can be so eager to feel heroic that they reward bad behavior in others. The result is more bad behavior, which a hero might interpret as a greater need for their rescue efforts. The codependent partner of an addict is the most familiar example. The spouse or parent ends up enabling the addiction, but she keeps doing it because rescuing others is the way her brain has learned to feel important.

Winning the love of a higher-status person is another widespread strategy for stimulating serotonin. We don't mix love and status consciously, but when a high-status person of the right gender notices you, your brain lights up. Even bonobos, the apes known for sexual dynamism, compete vigorously for high-status partners. Once that trophy partner is yours, however, your serotonin stops surging. It would surge again if you found an even higher-status love object. Probably you restrain the urge to do that, but it's easy to see others yielding to it. A superstar spouse makes a person feel good, and that wires the brain to expect good feelings by acquiring a superstar spouse again. Some people repeat the cycle despite the side effects.

Seeking Status Is Not a New Phenomenon

Serotonin disappointment is often blamed on "our society," but status frustrations are evident in every culture and time. In many cultures, cruelty to servants is accepted, and mothers-in-law dominate daughters-in-law with raw despotism. Tribal societies often have rigid dominance hierarchies, despite their egalitarian image. What looks like cooperation is often submission to learned expectations to avoid punishment. You may think you'd enjoy a serotonin high all the time if you lived in another time or place, but if you got there you'd find that the people there are still mammals, and you are too.

Social dominance grabs your attention because it promotes your genes in the state of nature. As soon as a mammal's immediate needs are met, its thoughts turn to social advancement. This includes everything from promoting the welfare of children to attracting a more powerful mate. Mammals that kept striving instead of being satisfied were more likely to survive and pass on their DNA. This is why we're so unsettled by flabby skin or a child's setbacks. Any small obstacle to getting respect feels like an obstacle to survival.

Everyone has a cousin who is doing better than they are. Your serotonin droops whenever you're reminded of that cousin, though you have plenty of good in your life. Perhaps you grew up hearing your parents make social comparisons and lament their own position. You may have wired yourself to take the one-down position and feel threatened instead of enjoying all the good that you have.

Serotonin Disappointment Can Be Healthy

Each brain seeks serotonin with pathways built during youth. There are no pathways that deliver endless serotonin, however. If you grew up around people who dominated you, your circuits prepared you for one kind of frustration. But if you grew up with a lot of admirers, you're wired for another kind of frustration. No matter what kind of expectations you're wired for, your quest for respect is disappointed sometimes. Managing that disappointment promotes your survival more than fleeing from it. When children fail to make the team or get a prom date, we teach them to try again. Seeking recognition is part of a healthy human life, despite the potential for disappointment.

You may protect yourself from serotonin disappointment by saying you don't care about status, but your neurochemicals respond to your status ups and downs whether or not you intend to. Your responses are shaped by time and place because you learn what gets respect in your world. If you lived in another time or place, you might have fought duels to defend your honor or stayed locked up at home to defend your honor. Today, you might pride yourself on your higher consciousness. You feel entitled to the one-up position because of your higher consciousness. When you see persons of lower consciousness getting respect, you may find yourself triggered in a way you think quite beneath you. And when you do get the respect you crave, it doesn't make you happy forever, despite your higher consciousness. Your brain is soon hatching plans to get more.

EXERCISE: WHEN DOES YOUR SEROTONIN DROOP?

If you were a big fish in a small pond, you would enjoy the one-up position all the time. But as soon as you heard of a bigger world with bigger fish, your serotonin would droop. A "do something" feeling would nag you until you found a way to advance your position. That serotonin droop keeps you seeking. It drove your ancestors to find a better way to skin a mammoth and let others know about it. You may be convinced you'll be happy forever when your big break comes, but each break you've had so far has left you longing for another break. It's easy to see this in others, but it helps to see it in yourself. Noticing your serotonin droop helps you avoid a sense of crisis when the one-up feeling eludes your grasp. Think of a time when:

You saw someone gain an advantage but they soon lost interest

_____

_____

_____

_____

You gained an advantage but you soon lost interest

_____

_____

_____

_____

You longed for a new advantage, and paid a high price for it

_____

_____

_____

_____

Happy Habits Help You Deal with Disappointment

If you saved your life by running up a tree when chased by a lion, your brain would learn to feel good about trees. Anything that transforms a bad feeling to a good feeling is a lifesaver from your mammal brain's perspective, and it builds a big pathway. If you lived in a world full of lions, you would always be scanning for trees. Since you don't, you instead scan for anything that once made you feel good in a moment when you felt bad. These are your "happy habits." They are not conscious choices, but pathways that create the expectation of feeling good. The good feelings don't last, of course, so we end up resorting to our happy habits a lot.

Distraction is often the core of a happy habit. Distraction can make you feel good just by interrupting the electricity in a bad loop. Distraction doesn't work if you smell a lion and distract yourself with perfume. But most of the time you are not facing a lion—you are facing the sting of disappointment. Anything that diverts your electricity feels like a lifesaver. If your stamp collection once distracted you from a bad feeling, your brain built a connection that expects relief from your stamp collection.

Why It's Difficult to Break Old Habits

I learned about the quirkiness of habits from a hypnotist who helps people quit smoking. He told me to imagine a fourteen-year-old boy at a party. The boy sees a girl he wants to talk to, but he's afraid. He tries a cigarette to steady his nerves, and it works! The girl returns his affection, and his happy chemicals flow. The reward is huge because it's so relevant to "reproductive success." The neurochemical spurt creates a huge link to his mammal brain that says: Cigarettes promote survival. Of course, the boy doesn't think this in words, but the next time he needs confidence in the face of a "survival challenge," his brain lights up the idea of smoking. With each cigarette, the pathway builds.

Years later, when he tries to quit smoking, the insecurity of the fourteen-year-old boy at a party surges up because it has nowhere to go without the cigarette pathway. His inner mammal feels like he's threatening his own survival when he resists the urge for a smoke. He must build a new happy habit in order to live without the old one.

Distract Yourself

Happy habits give your threatened feelings a place to go. If you felt disappointed by a bad grade in math long ago, whatever made you feel better built a pathway in your brain. If you went to a party and enjoyed it, your brain "learned" that a party makes you happy when you're feeling unhappy. Consciously, you know the party doesn't solve your math problems, but when the bad feeling returns, your party circuit is there. Each party makes it bigger.

Distraction is not a good survival strategy when action is needed. But when you feel miffed by a coworker at the next desk, you may be better off not acting. When your brain screams "do something," distraction gives you something to do. It protects you from fueling threatened feelings and rewards you with the sense that you're saving your life.

Side Effects of Habits

Every habit has side effects, and the more you indulge, the more side effects you get. At first, the consequences may be small, so it's easy to tell yourself "it's just one little cookie." "It's just one little drink." "It's just a little flirtation." "It's just a little splurge." "It's just a little anger." "It's just a little down time." "It's just a little risk." "It's just a little party." "It's just a little project." "It's just a little confidence-booster." "It's just a little lie." "It's just a little competition."

> **DO NOTHING!**
> You can stop a vicious cycle in one instant, simply by doing nothing. That teaches your brain that you will not actually die without the old habit. You learn that threatened feelings do not kill you. A virtuous circle begins the moment you do nothing and live with the threatened feeling instead of doing the usual something.

It would be nice to have a habit with no side effects, but happy chemicals evolved because of their consequences. When the consequences pile up enough to trigger your cortisol, you end up feeling threatened by the very behavior you use to relieve a threat. Now you're in a vicious cycle. You can probably think of ten vicious cycles in ten seconds: junk food, alcohol, love affairs, drugs, losing your temper, gaming, getting recognition, shopping, watching a screen, telling others what to do, withdrawing, career advancement, pleasing people, climbing mountains, rescuing people, smoking, dieting. (That's more than ten. I couldn't stop.) You know your happy habit can lead to pain, but when you try to feel better, you rely on the pathways you have. You feel like your survival is threatened when you resist.

How to Build a Virtuous Circle

The first step to happier habits is to do nothing when your cortisol starts giving you a threatened feeling. Doing nothing goes against your body's deepest impulse, but it empowers you to make changes in your life. Once you do nothing, you have time to generate an alternative. At first, no alternative looks as good as the habit does, but positive expectations build if you give a new pathway a chance to grow. Each time you divert your electricity in a new direction, you strengthen your new circuit. It all starts when you accept a bad feeling for a moment instead of rushing to make it go away.

It would be nice to have an alternative that feels good instantly. But instant good feelings are only triggered by behaviors that appeal to a mammal, like eating a hot fudge sundae, getting kissed by your teen idol, and accepting a standing ovation. Instant highs are not possible at every moment, so it's good to know that you can build a pathway to your happy chemicals with repetition even when something doesn't feel good instantly. When you know how your brain works, you can build more happy habits with fewer side effects. You can start a virtuous circle without being virtuous. The following chapters show how.

EXERCISE: VICIOUS CYCLES I HAVE KNOWN

Happy habits are pathways that relieved your threatened feelings in the past. When you stop a happy habit, that sense of threat resurges and you feel like you are threatening your own survival. If you yield to this impulse, the old circuit builds. If you do nothing, you create space for a new circuit to grow. Learn to notice the impulse to relieve threatened feelings with happy habits. When you know that your threatened feeling is just a connection between neurons, you free yourself to build new connections. Notice examples of:

Someone you know with a habit that relieves threatened feelings

_____

_____

_____

Someone's habit having side effects

_____

_____

_____

Your habit that relieves threatened feelings

_____

_____

_____

Your habit having side effects

_____

_____

_____

5 | HOW YOUR BRAIN WIRES ITSELF

Remaking Your Neural Connections

You were born with a lot of neurons but very few connections between them. Connections built as you interacted with the world around you, and they make you who you are. But you may want to remodel your circuits a bit. It seems like it should be easy because you built those circuits effortlessly in youth, but building new circuits in adulthood is surprisingly hard. Your old circuits are so efficient that avoiding them gives you the feeling that your survival is threatened. Any new circuits you build are flimsy by comparison. This is why change is difficult.

It helps to know how a brain actually builds its wiring, and that's what we'll discuss in this chapter. When you can appreciate how difficult it is to create new pathways, you can celebrate your persistence instead of berating your progress.

Five Ways Your Brain Builds Its Wiring

We mammals are born to create wiring instead of with wiring already established. Our circuits build as the world hits our senses and sends electricity to the brain. That electricity carves pathways that ease the flow of future electricity. Each brain is thus etched by its own experience. Following are five ways that experience physically changes your brain.

1. Experience Insulates Young Neurons

A neuron used repeatedly develops a fatty coating called myelin. This coating makes a neuron extremely efficient at conducting electricity, the way insulated wires are more efficient than bare wires. Myelinated circuits make a task feel effortless compared to doing it with slow, naked neurons. Myelinated neurons look white rather than gray, which is why we have "white matter" and "gray matter."

Much of your myelination happens by age two, as your body learns to see and hear and move. When a mammal is born, it has to build a mental model of the world around it in order to survive. But you don't need to relearn the experience that fire is hot and gravity makes you fall. That's why myelin surges at birth and trails off by age seven.

Myelination increases again at puberty. That's when a mammal needs to wire in new learning to improve its mating opportunity. Animals often move to a new group to mate, so they must learn to find food in new terrain and get along with new troop mates. Humans also seek mates in ways that involve learning the customs and survival strategies of a new tribe. The myelin surge of adolescence makes this possible. Natural selection built a brain good at rewiring its mental model of the world around puberty. We'll discuss more about the importance of what's learned in childhood and adolescence later in this chapter.

A MYELIN HIATUS

If you think myelin is "wasted" on the young, it helps to know there's a good evolutionary reason. For most of human history, people had babies as soon as they reached puberty. They were busy meeting the immediate needs of the children who kept coming. Adulthood was spent investing in new brains rather than rewiring old brains.

Anything you do repeatedly in your "myelin years" develops huge, efficient branches in your neural network. This is why child prodigies exist, and why little kids on ski slopes whoosh past you even though you're trying much harder than them. This is why new languages are hard to learn after puberty. You can learn new words, but you can't seem to find the words when you need to express yourself. That's because your new vocabulary is just skinny ungreased circuits. Your thoughts are generated by big myelinated circuits, so the electricity has trouble finding a place to flow.

Myelin also explains why it's hard to unlearn a circuit you'd rather do without. Your white matter is so efficient that you feel inept when you try to do without it. That inept feeling motivates you to return to the old path, even when it's not your best long-term survival choice. For example, if you've learned to feel strong by challenging other people, you may get yourself into trouble by challenging too much. But when you withhold your impulse to challenge, you might feel so weak that you blurt out a challenge. The opposite is true as well. You may have learned to feel safe by avoiding conflict, and you may get yourself into trouble by avoiding too much. But when you decide to challenge someone instead of avoiding conflict, you feel so unsafe that you quickly give up your new path and return to the old one.

The ups and downs of myelination can help you understand why certain current thought trends can be problematic:

- When you hear that teen brains aren't finished developing, remember that the brain does not mature automatically. It myelinates whatever it experiences. So if a teen gets rewards without doing the work, he "learns" that you can get rewards without effort. Some parents excuse a teen's bad behavior by saying "his brain isn't fully developed." But that's exactly why it's so important to shape the experiences they are soaking up. Letting a teen escape responsibility for his actions forms a brain that expects to escape responsibility for its actions.
- When you hear that an elderly brain can still learn, remember that the learning will not be easy, because myelination is so slow at this stage. Old brains build new learning only when a person engages in a lot of repetition. Service providers can help shape learning experiences, but they cannot build a circuit in someone else's brain.

2. Experience Makes a Synapse Efficient

A synapse is the gap between one neuron and the next. The electricity in your brain only flows if it reaches the end of a neuron with enough force to jump across that gap. These barriers help us filter important inputs from irrelevant buzz.

What it takes for electricity to spark a synapse is surprisingly complex. It's as if the tip of each neuron has a fleet of rowboats ready to ferry an electrical spark across the synapse to specially fitted docks on the next neuron. These rowboats get better at crossing over to their docks each time they're set into motion, and that's why experience improves the chances of a synapse firing. In a brain with 100 trillion synapses, experience helps channel your electricity in ways that promote survival.

You didn't decide consciously which synapses to develop. It happens in two ways:

1. Repetition, which develops a synapse gradually
2. Emotion, which develops a synapse instantly

BUILDING SYNAPSES WITHOUT EMOTION

Synapses can build without neurochemicals, but it takes a lot of repetition. For example, you can learn romantic words in a foreign language quite quickly, but learning verb conjugations usually requires dreary repetition. Romance triggers neurochemicals that build synapses quickly, but repetition gives you the power to build any synapse you decide is important. If a synapse is activated many times, it gradually learns to transmit an electrochemical signal efficiently, even without extra rowboats in the fleet.

Emotions are chemical molecules that can change a synapse immediately and permanently. It's as if you have more rowboats in the fleet harbored at that synapse. Whatever felt good or bad in your past developed synapses that will fire again more easily in the future. Here is a simple example: I used to carry popcorn on long plane trips and loved the tasty distraction. (Chewing is exercise!) But one day I chipped a tooth on my popcorn. Fear surged as I realized I was stranded in the air with no access to dentistry. The cortisol built strong new connections, and now I fear eating popcorn on a plane.

Your synapses built from the repetition and emotion of your past. You are intelligent because your neurons connected in ways that reflect the good and bad experiences you've had. Some of those experiences were turbo-charged by molecules of pleasure or pain, and some were frequently repeated. When patterns in the world match the patterns in your synapses, electricity flows and you feel like you know what's going on.

3. Only Neurons That Are Used Stick Around

Neurons that aren't used begin to wither in the brain of a two-year-old. That enhances intelligence, surprisingly. Pruning helps a toddler focus on the circuits he's built instead of spreading his attention everywhere the way a newborn does. A toddler can zoom in on things that felt good in his past, like a familiar face or the container that holds his favorite food. A toddler can also stay alert to things that felt bad in his past, such as a rough playmate or a closed door. The young brain is already relying on its own experience to steer toward meeting needs and away from potential threats.

The brain does much of its pruning between ages two and seven. This causes a child to link new experience to relevant past experience instead of storing each new experience as an isolated chunk. Richly interconnected networks are the source of our intelligence, and we create them by building new branches onto old trunks instead of building new trunks. So by the time you are seven, you are good at seeing what you have already seen and hearing what you have already heard.

You may think this is bad, so it's important to see the value. Imagine lying to a six-year-old. She believes you, because her brain takes in everything. Now imagine telling that lie to an eight-year old. She questions it because her brain compares new inputs to stored experience instead of just absorbing all new inputs. New circuits are harder to build at age eight, which motivates a child to rely on her existing circuits. Your trust in your old circuits makes it possible for you to detect a lie. This had tremendous survival value in a world where parents died young and children had to meet their own needs at an early age.

You spent your early years developing some neural networks while allowing others to atrophy. Some of your neurons got swept away like autumn leaves, and that streamlined your thought process. You added new knowledge, of course, but you did that in areas where your electricity already flowed. If you were born into a hunting tribe, for example, you easily added more useful hunting information, and if you were born into a farming tribe, you had solid farming circuits to build onto. You ended up with a brain honed to survive in the world you actually lived in.

The zip of electricity through your circuits gives you the feeling that things make sense. When the world doesn't fit your developed circuits, your electricity trickles so you have less confidence in your knowledge.

4. New Synapses Grow Between Neurons You Use

Each neuron can have many synapses because it can have many branches, or dendrites. New dendrites grow when there's a lot of electrical stimulation. As dendrites grow toward hot spots of electrical activation, they may get close enough for electricity to jump the gap. Thus a new synapse is born. When this happens, you have a connection between two ideas.

You don't feel your own synapses, but they're easy to observe in others. A person who likes dogs seems to connect everything to dogs, and a person who likes technology often connects things to technology. A person who likes politics seems to connect everything to her political views, and a religious person easily connects things to his religious beliefs. One person sees positive connections and another person sees negative connections.

Whatever connections you have, you don't experience them as tentacles grown by well-used neurons. You experience them as "the truth."

5. Emotion Receptors Grow or Atrophy

For electricity to cross a synapse, the dendrite on one side must release a chemical that arrives at a receptor on the other side. Each of our brain chemicals has a complex shape that fits its own special receptors the way a key fits a lock. When you feel flooded by emotion, you are releasing more chemicals than those receptors can process. You feel overwhelmed and disoriented until your brain builds more receptors. That's how you adapt when you are "going through something."

FIVE WAYS EXPERIENCE CHANGES YOUR BRAIN

1. Experience insulates young neurons with myelin, so they're superfast conductors of electricity.
2. Experienced synapses are better at sending electricity to neighboring neurons, so you're better at lighting up a path you've lit up before.
3. Neurons atrophy if they're not used, so you rely more heavily on the neurons you've used.
4. New synapses grow between neurons you use, so you make connections.
5. Receptors grow and atrophy, so it's easier to process the feelings you experience repeatedly.

When a receptor is not used for a while, it disappears, which leaves space for any new receptors you may need. Flexibility is good, but it also means that you must use your happy receptors or lose them.

Happy chemicals float around seeking receptors they fit into. That's how you "know" what you're happy about. A neuron fires because a happy-chemical key has opened a receptor lock, and that firing develops the neurons that tell you where to expect happiness in the future.

Finding Your Free Will

You don't always act on your neurochemical impulses because your prefrontal cortex can *inhibit* a response. It can even shift your attention from one activation pattern to another. We humans have the power to shift our attention from a circuit activated by the outside world to a circuit we activate internally. We are not powerless servants of our impulses because of this.

Your Limbic Brain and Cortex Work Together

When the information reaching your senses turns on your brain chemicals, it gets your attention. That's the job these chemicals evolved to do. You are always deciding whether to "go with the flow" or divert your electricity elsewhere. You either act on your neurochemical impulse or generate an alternative. Then you decide whether to act on the alternative. You go for it if it stimulates happy chemicals. If not, you generate another alternative. This is how your separate brain parts work together. Your cortex comes up with options and your limbic brain responds to them as good for you or bad for you. You do this so efficiently that you hardly notice.

Animals do it too, but in a way that only requires a small cortex. An animal is always choosing between competing impulses to seek rewards and avoid pain. A human brain associates these impulses with related circuits in long chains of associations. You can anticipate the future before responding to an impulse. But eventually, you shift from thinking to acting, and neurochemicals help you do that. Electricity flows through your neural pathways, but you always have the power to redirect the flow. This is the core of your free will.

For example, if my husband does something that gets on my nerves, I could allow myself to dwell on it. Then my circuits would spark, my chemicals would gush, and I could tell myself he is causing the fireworks. But I am free in every moment to shift my attention elsewhere.

Focusing Your Attention on Survival

Your attention is limited. If you invest it in one place, you have less to invest in alternatives. It takes little attention to follow a familiar path, but shifting to the unfamiliar makes heavy demands on your attention. You have to juice up the weak signals to make sense of them, which leaves you less electricity for other efforts. You are always deciding which use of your electricity best promotes your survival.

Imagine your ancestor spotting a lion on the savannah. To survive, he focuses intensely on the lion to see which way it's headed. At some point he decides to run, so he shifts his attention to the ground in front of him instead of the lion. You do this when changing lanes in traffic by shifting your attention between the rearview mirror and the cars themselves. Now imagine a person who spends most of his attention on web surfing. He is not conscious of deciding to invest his attention in that way. He often thinks of doing something else, but then a bad feeling comes up. A shift back to web surfing relieves the bad feeling, creating the impression that it promotes his survival. His connections facilitate this flow, but he is always free to shift his attention elsewhere.

The brain often generates conflicting impulses. You want to eat pizza and you don't want to. You want to write your opus and you don't want to. You want to call your mother and you don't want to. You are always deciding which impulse to act on and which to inhibit.

An ape is always doing that, too. When an ape sees a juicy mango, she wants it, but she also wants to avoid being bitten by the bigger ape next to her. She inhibits the impulse to grab while assessing all the survival-relevant information around her. You have more neurons than an ape, especially in the important prefrontal cortex. You can consider more options, and you can even generate options in your mind that you've never experienced in the sensory world. It all depends on where you direct your attention. When you don't direct, your electricity flows down the path of least resistance.

How Small Experiences Create Big Circuits

Before there was "education," and even before there was language, people learned survival skills from repetition and emotion.

Building Survival Circuits

A baby chimpanzee builds life skills while watching the world from his mother's lap. Before he knows what food is, he sees crumbs fall from her mouth. They land on her chest right in front of his eyes. He has the urge to grasp a crumb and put it in his mouth because his mirror neurons have registered his mother doing that. It takes several tries because his muscles haven't learned to grasp yet. He's not driven by hunger because he's fully nourished by her milk. When a crumb finally lands in his mouth, it feels good! His dopamine surges, and he makes a connection. The next time he sees a crumb, he expects more good feeling, so he goes for it. Without conscious intent, he builds the wiring that will enable him to meet his needs.

Mother chimps never feed solids to their children. If the little chimp wants to eat something besides milk, he has to get it himself. And he can, because he has built the essential circuits by the time he's big enough to need the extra nutrition. She doesn't show him or push him explicitly. He learns because food is rewarding, and because he has seen her choosing food over and over. When weaning time comes, he's wired to choose the plants she has chosen. By the time his mother is gone, he has the skills he needs to survive without her.

Researchers have found that chimpanzees can recognize more than a hundred different kinds of leaves. They even select leaves with medical properties when they are sick. But the reward that counts in a chimp's life is protein, such as nuts, insects, and meat. These foods are relatively difficult to obtain. Still, children are not provisioned. They only get the reward if they execute the skill.

A young chimp can take years to succeed at cracking open a nut. He gets interested because he tastes the crumbs his mother leaves in the shells of her nuts. His dopamine soars because the fat content is so much higher than the food he typically encounters. In the state of nature, good feelings surge when something is good for your survival. But when the young chimp tries to imitate his mother's nut-cracking movements, the darned thing doesn't open. He persists because dopamine gushes when big rewards are expected. He observes the nut-cracking efforts of others and tries again.

I once spent ten minutes watching a young capuchin monkey fail to crack a nut over and over. I was overwhelmed by an urge to "help." I looked for a zookeeper, and when I found one, she told me I shouldn't worry about it because the monkeys are well fed and this behavior is natural. If I were running the "education" of monkeys, they wouldn't learn survival skills and the species would die out.

Building Social Skills

Social skills are learned the same way a primate learns foraging skills. Sitting on mother's lap, he sees her interact with others. He sees her dominate some of the time and submit some of the time. He doesn't need to label these responses. His mirror neurons simply trigger fear when she fears, dominance when she dominates, and trust when she trusts. This builds pathways that guide him in his quest for good feelings and his avoidance of bad feelings. He begins to interact directly with others, and by the time he's grown, he's wired to survive within the social expectations of his troop.

Chimps are not born preprogrammed with necessary survival knowledge. Their mothers invest five years in each child before reproducing again. The survival of the mother's genes clearly benefits more from the extended nurturing than it would from having another child. But the young chimp's education is not guided by the mother's conscious intent. It's guided by the urge for the good feelings of dopamine, oxytocin, and serotonin, and the urge to avoid the bad feeling of cortisol.

Human Learning

These neurochemicals guide our early learning as well. We learn some things consciously, like long division and punctuation, but we learn a lot from our neurochemical responses. The two strategies often work together because we feel good when we master a skill with conscious intent. We feel bad when we fall short of a goal we consciously pursue. Without our knowing it, the quest to feel good builds circuits that prepare us to meet our needs.

This is most evident when we speak of a person's "passion." Consider the child who watches a doctor cure a sick family member and then decides to become a doctor. That child built a big circuit because a life-and-death experience triggers a big neurochemical surge. We are not always aware of the neurochemical origins of our passions. They're built in childhood with a child's view of survival. For example, if you got respect from your basket-weaving teacher, the surge of good feeling might motivate you to devote your life to basket weaving. If you grow up watching rock stars get respect, you might long to be a rock star. In adulthood you might realize that your passions do not promote survival, but by then the major highways to your happy chemicals are already built.

People often complain that "we don't learn from experience," but we do—it just may not be in the way you imagine. Experiences that are neurochemical or repeated build circuits that endure. Experiences in youth build supercircuits. If you invest a lot of energy seeking approval from people who reject you, that habit probably helped you survive in your youth. If you invest yourself in conflicts with authority figures, you probably got rewards or avoided pain by doing that in your youth. If you have a circuit that gets you into trouble, you can be sure that it got rewards or avoided pain in your past.

Discovering What Triggers the "On" Switch of Your Happy Chemicals

By the time you reach adulthood, you have a neural network that tells you what is good for you. It is not the network you'd design today if you started with a blank sheet of paper. It's the tangle you connected one neuron at a time from the moment your senses began taking in information.

The Burden of Numerous Neurons

Genes have a role to play. An amazing example is the laboratory mouse that started digging the first time she touched dirt. Her ancestors lived in cages for thirty to sixty generations, but she hit the ground digging, and she dug burrows that were much like those of her wild counterparts. The circuits for this survival behavior seem to be inborn.

But mice brains are different from ours. Their cortex is tiny, which means their ability to learn from experience is tiny. Our cortex is huge because we are designed to fill it with acquired knowledge. We are not meant to run on preloaded programs.

Every creature in nature runs on as few neurons as possible because neurons are metabolically expensive. They consume more oxygen and glucose than an active muscle. It takes so much energy to keep a neuron alive that they make it harder to survive—unless you really get your money's worth out of them. Natural selection gave humans a gargantuan number of neurons, which means we must use them with gargantuan advantage over inborn knowledge. We are designed to trust the neural networks we've built. This is why it's so hard to ignore them, even when they lead us astray.

You Do Most of Your Neural Learning in Childhood

Childhood evolved to give a creature time to build its neural networks. The length of a creature's childhood is directly correlated with the size of its cortex, and a human childhood is by far the longest. Small-brained creatures have short childhoods because their operating system boots up quickly. A mouse is a parent by the time it's two months old. A giraffe "hits the ground running" because it crashes four feet from the womb to the ground, and in a few weeks it can do almost everything an adult can do. Primates have a very long childhood by comparison. A monkey's childhood is about three times as long as a gazelle's. An ape's childhood is triple that of a monkey. A human childhood triples an ape's. The more neurons you have to maintain, the longer it takes to connect them in ways that promote survival.

Childhood is metabolically expensive because it reduces the number of offspring a mother can have. But natural selection does not favor shorter childhoods as you might expect. Longer childhoods evolved over time because natural selection rewards survival skills learned from life experience.

Childhood frees an organism from the burden of meeting its needs so it can learn to meet its needs gradually by interacting with its environment. Animals with short periods of early dependency need inborn survival skills, so they can only survive in the ecological niche of their ancestors. They typically die outside that niche. Humans are born ready to adapt to whatever niche they're born into. But once you build those adaptations, you're designed to rely on them as if your life depends on it. This is why it's hard to unlearn a happy-chemical strategy once you've learned it.

Look Back at Your Childhood to Find the Source of Your Circuits

We don't usually associate childhood with survival skills. After all, children don't learn how to get a job with good benefits, or a mate that will impress your friends. We often presume childhood habits have nothing to do with adult life. But early experience tells you how to feel good and avoid feeling bad, and that is the navigation system that pilots a brain through adult challenges. When your boss makes you feel bad, you may want to fight or flee, but your navigation system reminds you that you need support, so you reconcile with your boss. You are always weighing your options with the network of connections built by your life experience.

Sophisticated adults don't imagine themselves navigating with childhood circuits, but if you examine your likes and dislikes, you will see where they came from. I discovered a curious example in myself when I noticed that I get excited about opportunities to choose colors. Since this is not an obvious survival skill, I tried to make sense of it. Early experiences involving color flooded back to me. When I was twelve, my mother inherited $2,000 (about $15,000 in today's money). It was a lot of money to my mother, and it came from the father who had abused and abandoned her, so she decided to spend it redecorating. She showed me color swatches and asked my opinion.

This felt good because my mother didn't respect my opinion very often. The happy chemicals told my brain that this was important survival information. I didn't consciously say "choosing colors is a way to get respect"; I didn't need to. The respect simply triggered serotonin, which connected all the neurons active at that moment.

More important, my mother was happy and my mirror neurons took it in. She was not happy often, so this was significant information for my brain. Without a conscious interest in decorating, I wired myself to expect more good feeling in this particular way. Of all the ways to feel good in the world, the ones you've already connected are the ones that get your attention.

Curiously, my brain had already been primed for this information. When I was in elementary school, my mother gave me a lot of paint-by-number kits. I also made art by gluing mosaic tiles and colored pebbles in the manner popular in the early 1960s. These crafts gave me a feeling of accomplishment and helped me focus on something other than the unpleasantness around me. Repetition and emotion trained my brain to sift and sort colors and feel good about it. Though picking colors is not an important survival skill, my happy chemicals were wired by my unique experience. Of course, I had many other experiences, and together they tell me where to expect rewards and where to expect pain.

When I was in high school, I wanted to be an interior decorator when I grew up. Then I got to college and learned that materialism is bad, and "girl jobs" are bad. Saving the world is good, I learned, so I dropped the decorating idea fast. I thought I had become a better person, but now I know I was just mirroring my professors the way I had mirrored my mother.

When I got an apartment, I started decorating it. I moved a lot in my twenties, and each time, the joy of decorating a new place eased the pain of starting over. When I finally put down roots, I had a curious urge to redecorate again and again. After a while, I realized that another remodeling project would not really meet my needs. So I set out to understand the urge instead of acting on it. I traced the links between one experience and another until the connections made sense. Then I realized that my happy-chemical pathways are just accidents rather than eternal truths. My brain connected decorating to survival because it connected my mother to survival.

When I figured this out, I looked at color in a new way—as a tool I could use to add pleasure to my work. I enjoy adding color to my website, my slide presentations, my meals, and my clothing. I allow myself to linger over details I'm wired to enjoy. I make good use of the happy-chemical infrastructure I have, which activates my happy chemicals without redecorating. I redirect my circuits toward today's needs instead of the needs of my past.

We all end up with quirky circuits like mine because we build on the connections that are already there. Our happy chemicals pathways feel important so it's hard to realize that they are just accidents. Anything that turns on your happy chemicals feels precious, which can lead to behaviors that are hard to make sense of. It can even lead to behaviors that are destructive. Though you can't just delete an old circuit, you can connect it in new ways that are better suited to your present reality. It won't happen effortlessly the way it did when you were young. But repetition and emotion can make it happen.

The Role of Happy Chemicals in Social Learning

A mammal's survival depends on social skills as much as physical skills. Small brains are born with the social skills they need, while big brains build social skills from repetition and emotion.

Social skills are essential to reproductive success. Though reproduction is not your definition of success, it's what mattered in the world our brains evolved in. The skills involved in reproductive success vary for males and females:

- A female can only birth a limited number of offspring, and in the past many of those perished before puberty. The survival of a female's genes depends on her ability to keep her children alive. Social skills can help a female get protection, nutrition, and better paternal genes.
- A male mammal can promote his genes by creating more offspring and investing less in each one. The quantity strategy rewards males skilled at attracting females and competing with other males.

The male and female strategies overlap, of course, and evolution tends to increase the overlap.

For both genders, getting respect from your peers promotes survival. Monkey studies show that individuals with more social alliances have more mating opportunities and more surviving offspring. So it's not surprising that the brain built by natural selection seeks social trust by rewarding it with a good feeling.

A young mammal builds social skills without effort or intent as it seeks ways to feel good and avoid feeling bad. Children build social skills without insight into their long-term needs. A child seeks social support to meet immediate needs, and when it succeeds, happy chemicals flow. That paves expectations about future social support.

Social Learning in Your Childhood and Adolescence

Anything that works gets wired in, even behaviors that could be counterproductive in the long run. If a bad behavior gets a reward, a young brain tags that behavior as useful for survival. If a child gets support when he is aggressive, and the support disappears when he's cooperative, a brain can easily learn that aggression is a good survival strategy. If a child gets rewarded when she's sick, and she loses rewards as she gets well, lasting links get built. Your brain doesn't learn from parenting experts and etiquette manuals. It learns from neurochemical ups and downs. Each time you felt rewarded or threatened, you added to the infrastructure that tells you where to expect respect, acceptance, and trust in the future.

Adolescence added a layer to your infrastructure. Whatever won respect or attention in your teen years developed big fat circuits because you experience more myelination then. Likewise, any threats to your respect and attention during these myelin years made a lasting impression. Any success at building social alliances built a pathway, and any threats to your social alliances built a pathway too.

Your social circuits are richly interconnected with your other circuits. Social learning even affects basic physiological functions like walking, eating, and even breathing. For example, an infant learns to regulate his breathing when he's held against his mother's chest and he feels her breathe. A newborn lacks a fully developed breathing response, so even breathing requires social support to develop properly.

Self-management is also affected by social learning. Children learn to manage their neurochemistry when they experience the responses of those around them. Adolescence adds a layer of self-management circuits, as we experience new social rewards, new social pain, and new social influences. These circuits shape our responses in the present, whether or not we remember the experiences that created them.

EXERCISE: WHAT ARE YOUR EARLY PATTERNS?

List early experiences of happiness and unhappiness, and notice the circuits they paved:

Before age eight

_____

_____

_____

In adolescence

_____

_____

_____

List early experiences that were repeated often and notice the circuits they paved:

Before age eight

_____

_____

_____

In adolescence

_____

_____

_____

Remodeling Your Neural Pathways

Most adults end up with some circuits they'd rather not have. And most people wish they could have more happy chemicals with fewer side effects. You cannot build new circuits in the effortless way it happened the first time. But you *can* build them with repetition and emotion.

Rebuilding via Repetition vs. Emotion

Emotion is a Catch-22. Anything that feels good now will have side effects later. Good feelings exist because of their side effects, thanks to natural selection. So the quest to feel good does not always lead to survival improvements. It can lead to weight gain when you quit smoking, or a new phobia when you conquer an old phobia. Emotion works fast, but it brings trouble.

Repetition works slowly, but it can build behaviors with fewer side effects. If you expose yourself to something over and over, it can "grow on you." You can come to like things that are good for you even though you don't like them instantly.

But who wants to repeat something over and over if it doesn't feel good? Usually, people don't, especially when they're already feeling bad. This is why we rely on the circuits built by accidents of experience. Your accidents will shape you unless you start repeating things by choice.

Alas, repetition can be harder than you expect. It feels boring, in common parlance, to do things that don't feel connected to your immediate needs. Without emotion to flag a behavior as "good for you," your brain tends to dismiss it as unimportant. Without happy chemicals to spark the action, a new pathway is hard to fire. But you can do it anyway.

An Example: Sticking with It

Here's a simple example. Fred wants to control his alcohol use. He decides to substitute a new pleasure with fewer side effects. He looks around for something that can grow on him, and remembers how he enjoyed sketching when he was young. He resolves to take out his sketchpad every time he feels like drinking. The goal is not to be good at sketching but to be good at shifting his attention elsewhere when he thinks of drinking. Of course, Fred doesn't feel like sketching when he longs for a drink. In fact, he feels bad as he sketches and thinks about what he's missing. But he resolves to live with the bad feelings for a while. He plans to do this for two months because he has a big event on the calendar then.

At first, he hates his sketches and he hates the feeling of denying himself a drink. But he sticks to his plan whether or not it feels good immediately. After a while, his sketching time starts to feel like a gift rather than a burden. Fred learns that the unhappy feelings soon pass. Best of all, he discovers the joy of being alert and responsible. Before the two months are over, he stops looking at the calendar. His sketching circuit has grown big enough to compete with his alcohol circuit. Now he knows how to feel good without a drink. He knows it physically as well as cognitively. Sketching was simply a way to do something once his "do something" feeling started flowing. Fred is so pleased with his remodel that he can't wait to build another new circuit.

An Example: Finding What Works for You

You can train your brain to feel good in new ways. Start by designing the new circuit you'd like to have. It may take a little trial and error to find the new habit that works for you with minimum side effects. Consider Louise, who wants a new job but can't get herself to push through a sustained job search. She feels bad about her career prospects and escapes those bad feelings with a variety of habits. She decides to break the vicious cycle by learning to feel good about the act of job-hunting. She sets the goal of applying to two jobs a day and developing her career skills for two hours a day.

On Day One, she meets her goal, but feels curiously awful. She eats an ice cream to escape the awful feeling, but finds herself craving another ice cream. The next day, she looks for a different way to feel good. She calls a friend after completing her task, but finds that talking about her career doesn't really make her feel better. On Day Three, it's dark by the time her career advancement work is over, and she decides to celebrate with a night on the town. The next morning, it's hard to get started. She thinks of all the disappointment she's endured and all the things she'd rather be doing. She decides to remove herself from temptation by going to a coffee shop while she works on her applications. By the time she finishes the coffee, she's in the middle of her second application. It seems to just flow. The next day, she heads for a coffee and brims with career-speak. The following day, she finds herself actually looking forward to her coffee-plus-accomplishment routine, and by the next week she has figured out how to make luscious coffee drinks at home. When six weeks have gone by, she's under consideration for a number of jobs, has a wealth of interview experience, and new confidence in her skills. Most important, she has experienced good feelings, which wired her to expect more good feelings when she thinks about doing more.

The point is not that coffee solves problems. The point is that inertia is hard to overcome. A habit that will feel good later is hard to start now. Louise and Fred found a way to trigger positive expectations without harmful side effects. With trial and error, you can find a habit that works for you.

Every brain is different. Some people would have a whole pot of coffee and never push the submit button on those job applications. Some people would love sketching but spill wine all over their sketchpad. You can experiment with alternatives before you commit for forty-five days. But if you keep starting over, your new habit will never build. After a few test runs, you need to keep repeating your new habit whether or not it feels good.

6 | NEW HABITS FOR EACH HAPPY CHEMICAL

Specific Suggestions to Get You Started

We are lucky to live in a time when our brain is increasingly well understood. You can learn to turn on your happy chemicals in new ways. No one can do this for you and you cannot do it for someone else. This chapter outlines specific suggestions for new roads to dopamine happiness, endorphin happiness, oxytocin happiness, and serotonin happiness. The abundance of choices will help you find a path you can believe in. Then you can wire it into your brain by repeating it for forty-five days without fail. Once you've built a new habit, you will be so pleased with your power over your brain that you will want to build another.

New Dopamine Habits

Celebrate Small Victories

You have some success every day, so commit to finding it and say, "I did it!" You will not conduct a symphony at Carnegie Hall every day. You will not lead starving hordes into the Promised Land every day. Adjust your expectations so you can be pleased with something you actually do. This doesn't mean you are lowering your expectations, or "full of yourself" or losing touch with reality. It means you are lingering on your gains the way you already linger on your losses.

Celebrating small steps triggers more dopamine than saving it up for one big achievement. Big accomplishments don't make you happy forever, so if you always tie happiness to a far-off goal, you may end up frustrated. Instead, learn to be happy with your progress. You will not be celebrating with champagne and caviar each day. You will be giving yourself permission to have a feeling of accomplishment. This feeling is better than external rewards. It's free, it has no calories, and it doesn't impair your driving. You have a small victory every day. Why not enjoy it?

> **NO SUCCESS IS TOO SMALL**
> Do not undermine your good feeling by apologizing to yourself for the triviality of the accomplishment. Just enjoy the split second of triumph and move on. It's just a spark, but if you ignite it every day, you will be your own best spark plug.

At first, it might feel silly to look for reasons to pat yourself on the back, and the reasons you come up with might make you uncomfortable. Still, commit to doing this whether or not it feels good. You can decide to be worthy of your own applause and enjoy the feeling, even if just for a split second. If it feels fake or forced, that's normal, because the circuits that berate your accomplishments feel strong and true.

Celebrating small accomplishments is a valuable skill, because big things come from many small steps. You won't take those steps if you are just running on the fumes of the last big thing.

Finally, your daily triumph will feel better if it doesn't depend on one-upping someone. If you have to win in ways that make someone lose, you limit yourself and end up with side effects. You can celebrate what you are creating instead of just who you are defeating.

Take Small Steps Toward a New Goal

It doesn't take much time or money to step toward a goal. Just commit ten minutes a day and you will feel momentum instead of feeling stuck. Ten minutes is not enough to move mountains, but it's enough to approach the mountain and see it accurately. Instead of dreaming about your goal from afar, you can gather the information you need to plan realistically. Your goals might change as your information grows. You might even learn that your fantasy goal would not make you happy. Those ten-minute investments can free you from unnecessary regret and help you find a hill you can actually climb. Your ten-minute efforts can define manageable steps so you're not just waiting for huge leaps that never come.

> **TAKE ACTION, DON'T JUST DAYDREAM**
> Spend your time on concrete action. Don't spend it fantasizing about quitting your day job or pressuring others to help you. It's not their goal. Dig into practical realities instead. Do this faithfully for forty-five days and you will have the habit of moving forward.

If you think you can't spare ten minutes a day, consider the time you already spend dreaming of what you'd rather be doing. You can use that time to research the necessary steps. You will get a dopamine feeling each day as those steps come into view. You will start to expect that dopamine feeling and look forward to it. You will learn to feel that it's possible to transform a dream into reality with steady effort.

When your ten minutes is over, go back to living in the present. Do not make a habit of focusing constantly on the future.

Divide an Unpleasant Task Into Small Parts

Everyone has a dreaded task they'd rather forget about. It might be the mess inside your closets or the mess inside an important relationship. Commit to spending ten minutes a day on your dreaded task. You don't need to have the solution when you start, only the willingness to keep stepping.

You may think it's impossible to clean out closets or renegotiate relationships in ten-minute chunks. But if you wait for grand solutions, you will languish for quite a long time. Instead, go to that closet, pull out one chunk of mess, and sort it out for ten minutes. Go to that yucky relationship riddled with disappointment and plant goodwill for ten minutes. Don't let a day go by without tackling another chunk. Keep it up for forty-five days and you will be comfortable tackling the annoyances that stand in the way of making your life better. Of course, you can't control other people the way you can control the contents of your closet. But you will replace a bad feeling with a good feeling if you keep trying. And you will keep trying because your positive expectations trigger dopamine.

Your dreaded task may miraculously resolve itself in less than forty-five days! If so, don't stop. Find another painful mess so you keep going for forty-five more days. That's what builds the habit of facing tough challenges in small increments instead of being intimidated by them. Remember to feel good about what you've done each day. Soon, you'll have the habit of tackling obstacles and feeling rewarded by it.

Keep Adjusting the Bar

Good feelings flow when the level of challenge you face is "just right." If a basketball hoop is too low, you get no pleasure from scoring points. If it's too high, you have no reason to try. Effort is fun when you expect a reward for your effort but it's not certain. You can adjust the hoops in your life and make things fun.

For forty-five days, experiment with lowering the bar in areas where you have set yourself impossible goals and raising the bar in places where you've set it so low that you feel no reward. If you feel you have no choice between frozen dinners and gourmet banquets, define a moderate cooking goal and start your forty-five days now. If you feel you have no choice between sitting on the couch and walking the red carpet, try going out in a middle-of-the-road way, and then try another way.

EXERCISE: WHAT ARE YOUR NEW DOPAMINE STRATEGIES?

Remodeling projects that can work for me:

Celebrate small victories

_____

_____

_____

Take steps toward a new goal

_____

_____

_____

Divide an unpleasant task into small parts

_____

_____

_____

Keep adjusting the bar

_____

_____

_____

New Endorphin Habits

Laugh

Laughing stimulates endorphin as it spontaneously convulses your innards. Find out what makes you laugh, and make time for it. A big *ha-ha* laugh is necessary to trigger endorphin—sneering at people you disdain doesn't do it. Nor does laughing on the outside, although that might prime the pump. It can be hard to find what triggers your laughs, but you can commit to keep sampling comedy until you get your daily laugh.

Laughter is a release of fear. Imagine laughing with relief after a close call with a snake. Social risks are more common than predator risk in modern life, and we often fear expressing a socially unacceptable emotion. Social shunning is a real survival threat in the state of nature, so we are wired to take these things seriously. Comedians often express socially risky feelings. When they survive, the part of you that fears shunning laughs with relief. You can think of laughing as creating safety instead of thinking it's frivolous.

You can enjoy more relief if you put it at the top of your priority list for forty-five days. Don't give up if it takes a bit of trial and error. I often think jokes are "not funny," but I have found a local improv troop that always seems hilarious to me. So I make time for it, a lot.

Cry on Occasion

Crying releases endorphin because of the physical exertion. I do *not* suggest making a habit of crying—it comes with a lot of cortisol too. But most adults habitually squelch the urge to cry, and that creates tension. Unsquelching relieves the tension. A few minutes of crying can relieve a bad feeling that you've squelched for years.

You can't cry on cue, nor should you make a goal of crying. But for forty-five days, you can make space to cry if the urge arises. The important step is to notice tension in your chest, back, abdomen, and throat when you are resisting the urge to cry. This tension will loosen when you pay attention to it. Unpleasant memories or sensations may also come up when you lower your guard. Sometimes it's useful information, and sometimes it's an old response that you've held in for years. If you feel like crying, don't block it with the idea that it's weak and foolish. The unpleasantness of the moment will pass and the nice loosening will remain.

It bears repeating that a crying habit is not the goal. The daily goal is to notice the tension between your crying reflex and your don't-be-a-crybaby reflex. For forty-five days, you can commit to accepting this tension instead of running from it. The feeling may be so familiar that it's hard to notice. Watching sad movies may activate that circuit for you. Other people's tragedies trigger your mirror neurons, and a stranger's threatened feelings may be easier to accept at first than your own.

Crying is our chief survival skill at birth, but over time we learn that crying can leave us worse off. We learn alternatives, but sometimes nothing works and you run out of alternatives. Cortisol keeps surging and you feel like a trapped animal. Your cortex can distract you away from this feeling, but your muscles may keep armoring you with trapped-animal tension. You can wear out your squelching muscles like any other overused body part. Crying can be physical therapy for a tensed-up diaphragm.

Exercise Differently

Varying your exercise routine is a good way to trigger endorphin. It takes strain to trigger endorphin, and if you keep straining the same place, you risk injury. If you work new places with new exercise, moderate exertion can stimulate endorphin.

Your body has three layers of muscles. When you vary your exercise, you give the neglected, constricted layers more attention. Since they're weak, they have to work harder, so you stimulate development where it's needed instead of going overboard on the parts you overuse. Chasing an endorphin high is not worth the risk of wearing out a part and needing a parts replacement. Variety is a great alternative.

If you're a person who doesn't exercise at all, everything you do will be something different. If you're already athletic, you may hate the uncoordinated feeling you get when you try something new. You may see it as a setback, when it's actually strengthening your weakest link. Free yourself from performance anxiety for forty-five days. You may like it so much that you want to try another variation for another forty-five days.

Stretch

Endorphin is also stimulated when you stretch. Everyone can add stretching to their daily routine, because you can do it while you're watching TV, waiting in line, or talking on the phone. Mild stretching brings circulation into constricted areas. Stop before you feel pain. Just because a little is good doesn't mean a lot is better. If you stretch every day for forty-five days, you will come to enjoy it so much that you will look forward to doing it every day.

Stretching is not just about arms and legs. Sample classes that introduce deeper stretches without hurting yourself. The point is not to push harder on the usual spots but to stretch spots you didn't know you had, such as the muscles between your ribs. Don't forget to stretch your toes, fingers, and even ears.

Slow movement is an essential variation on this theme. Tai chi and Qi Gong are so slow that you may think they're not real exercise. But super-slow movement is more of a workout than it seems. It forces you to use muscles evenly, activating the weaker muscles instead of letting the dominant ones take over. Commit to doing something that doesn't look like "real exercise" for forty-five days, and you will feel the difference.

Make Exercise Fun

Consider switching to a fun exercise for forty-five days. An exercise that triggers your happy chemicals helps motivate you toward more vigorous exertion. There are endless ways to make exercise fun. I took a waltzing class and was amazed at how hard I worked. Many people make exercise a social activity, from team sports to chatty hikes. It's fun to exercise with music or an enjoyable audio book. Novelty also makes things fun: My yoga teacher makes the class completely different every week. Biking or hiking to new destinations is stimulating. Finally, gardening has an extrinsic reward, which motivates many people to keep exerting. Adding fun to exercise can help you persist.

EXERCISE: WHAT ARE YOUR NEW ENDORPHIN STRATEGIES?

Remodeling projects that can work for me:

Laugh

_____

_____

_____

Cry

_____

_____

_____

Exercise differently

_____

_____

_____

Stretch

_____

_____

_____

Make exercise fun

_____

_____

_____

Building New Oxytocin Circuits

Build on "Proxy" Trust

Social trust is hard to create, so people often use proxies. Animals, crowds, and digital friends are proxies that can stimulate good feelings of social trust without the complications of human bonds. The oxytocin is less than with live personal contact, of course. But proxies can expand the foundation for future trust.

Proxy trust is comfortable because there's less risk of disappointment. Animals don't betray you, large crowds don't judge you, and digital friends are always available. Direct human trust always comes with the risk of disappointed expectations and feelings of betrayal. Those bad feelings built circuits that fire when you think about trusting again. Your neurochemical alarm bells ring and your brain presumes there's a good reason. But if you give up on direct interpersonal trust, your brain feels that something is missing. And it is: Oxytocin is missing.

Start with small steps that don't trip your alarm. Every time you feel good about an animal, a crowd, or a digital relationship, tell yourself "I am creating this good feeling." It may sound silly or self-centered, but knowing that you are creating it gives it a chance to grow. There will always be reasons for distrust to grow, so a source of balance is precious.

Notice your trusting feelings from any source for forty-five days, and you will build a foundation that can ignite more.

Place Stepping Stones

Maybe there's someone you want to trust, but you can't bridge the divide. It's good to know you can build trust with a long series of very small interactions. Individuals or groups with an unfortunate history cannot always wipe the slate clean all at once. Intermediate steps build trust gradually. The stepping stones can be placed so close together that neither party risks a big betrayal. Each step need only create positive expectations about the next step rather than resolve the whole problem. Each small experience of trust stimulates the good feeling of oxytocin, which connects neurons that help trigger more.

Divorce lawyers use this strategy to help a couple reach agreement. You might try it with that person who is "ruining your life." Initiate a very small interaction, and if that proceeds without disaster, do it again. The goal is not to trust blindly and get disappointed. The goal is to build positive expectations.

Coexisting without trust is bad, but getting burned again is worse. So instead of taking a leap of faith with that crazy neighbor or the coworker who stabbed you in the back, you can find steps that are comfortable. For forty-five days, craft reciprocal exchanges that build stepping stones toward trust with difficult people. You can't predict the results since you can't control others. But you will expand your sense of control over the trust bonds in your life. This is hard work, and it may not feel good in the short run. But in the long run, it builds confidence that you can do something about those thorns in your side.

You might start by just making eye contact with that person who's making your life difficult. The next day, you could comment on the weather, and add a smile the day after that. It could take a week to build up to a shared chuckle about traffic, and even that may stir up bad feelings that are curiously strong. But you will continue making neutral contact—neither venting anger nor rushing to please. In forty-five days, you will have built a new shared foundation. You may always need to limit your trust in this person, but you will be able to relax in his presence the way gazelles relax in a world full of lions.

Be Trustworthy

Oxytocin works both ways. When other people trust you, it feels good whether or not you trust them. You can enjoy more oxytocin by creating opportunities for people to trust you.

Handle this strategy with care—you do not want to be the rescuer of everyone you know forty-five days from now. Your goal is simply to feel the pleasure of another person's trust for a moment each day. Of course, you can't force other people to trust you, and it may take more than a moment to extend yourself in ways that build trust. Do not spend a lot of time seeking approval. Simply honor your commitments, and then pause to enjoy being a person who honors her commitments. It may sound self-important, but the circuit it builds is the foundation of future trust. So plan to honor your commitments scrupulously for forty-five days.

Create a Trust Verification System

You can practice the old adage "trust, but verify." Monitor results. Count your change. Check up on people. That may sound harsh, but verifying makes it possible to develop trust with strangers. If you're too nice to verify, you get stuck inside the safe harbor of people you already trust.

To venture beyond, you have to interact with people whose trustworthiness is unknown. By trusting and verifying, new trust can grow. If you do it for forty-five days, you can't predict what others will do, but you can build confidence in your ability to extend your trust circle. Instead of being confined to the niche where you can trust everyone, you have a tool for taking controlled risks.

Do not grow your circle by trusting people who are not trustworthy. The goal is not to trust as an end in itself, but to gather information about good places to trust. You succeed whether or not the other person shortchanges you, because you build trust in your own verification plan. Celebrate that each day, whether your trust is rewarded or disappointed.

Natural selection rewarded those who fanned out from familiar turf. In the animal world, young males are often ousted from their natal groups, or they leave on their own initiative because they're excluded from mating opportunities. They experience huge cortisol stress when they leave their trust networks for parts unknown, according to excretory samples taken in the wild. This stress intensifies when a new troop rejects them. But the seekers don't give up. They keep trying to build trust bonds, because it feels great when they succeed.

Get a Massage

Massage stimulates oxytocin. You don't have to spend a lot of money to have a daily massage. Here are some other options:

- Start a reciprocal exchange with a massage buddy.
- Build the skill in a community-education class so you can absorb the enthusiasm of your classmates.
- Try self-massage, which is surprisingly effective, too. The Qi Gong self-massage technique requires no special strength and it's easy to learn from a video.

Once you create the habit of stimulating your oxytocin in this way, it's a pleasure you will always have available.

EXERCISE: WHAT ARE YOUR NEW OXYTOCIN STRATEGIES?

Remodeling projects that can work for me:

Build on "proxy" trust

_____

_____

_____

Place stepping stones

_____

_____

_____

Be trustworthy

_____

_____

_____

Build a trust verification system

_____

_____

_____

Get a massage

_____

_____

_____

Building New Serotonin Circuits

Express Pride in What You've Done

Pride is complicated. Applause-seeking can have bad side effects, but when you get no recognition from others, something feels wrong. You could applaud yourself, but the brain is not easily tricked by hollow self-respect. It wants respect from others because that has survival value. Alas, there is no guaranteed safe way to get this serotonin boost. Social recognition is unpredictable and fleeting. But you can stimulate your serotonin without being "a jerk." Simply express pride in something you've done once a day.

Pride is a rudder that helps you navigate opportunities to get social recognition. It helps you steer between the opposite extremes of constant approval-seeking and cynical dejection.

Taking pride in yourself means more than just thinking it silently. It means daring to say, "Look what I did!" to another living soul. Asking others to respect your accomplishment is risky because you may be disappointed. People often protect themselves by insisting that social respect doesn't matter or that it's hopelessly unfair. But these rationales don't soothe the mammal brain's longing for the sense of security that social respect brings.

So for forty-five days, say "look what I did" to someone else once a day. You will expect a positive reaction, and if you don't get it, you will learn that it doesn't kill you. The next day you will crow with positive expectations again. It's hard to overcome negative expectations. It's natural to have concerns about the "right" way to crow. But if you keep trying for forty-five days, you will wire in the feeling of social respect.

KEEP AT IT

Many of the people we admire today got little respect while they were alive, but they kept working anyway. Do not assume that people who accomplish things have a perpetual cheering squad. It would be nice if that adulation just came to you, but keep going if it doesn't.

Ironically, people who get public adulation often complain about it. They feel trapped, longing to do something different, but fearful of losing the applause they have.

Whether you get a lot of social regard or a little, your brain will keep longing for it. That's what your mammal brain does.

And that's why you need the skill of taking pride in your own accomplishments instead of waiting around for applause.

If you focus on your shortcomings, you tend to overlook any applause you already have. You may be getting quiet respect that is not expressed as audible applause. That's why it's useful to expect appreciation once a day, even if you have to force yourself. It allows you to take in what is already there.

Enjoy Your Social Position in Each Moment

Believe it or not, your social position changes constantly. One minute you feel like you're in the subordinate position and the next minute you find yourself in the dominant position in relation to those you focus on. You hate the subordinate position, but when you're dominant, that frustrates you too. You can learn to enjoy the advantages of wherever you are instead of focusing on the frustrations.

You may think equality would make you happy, but the closer you get to it, the more your brain finds tiny differences to dwell on. When mammals gather, each brain seeks the good feeling of being dominant. You can easily see this in others, but when your brain does it, it feels like you're just seeking what you deserve. Your inner mammal will constantly find ways that you have been undervalued and this can make you miserable even in a rather good life. You will be much happier if you relax and enjoy wherever you find yourself.

You have built expectations about social rivalry from your past experience. The frustrations and disappointments of your past built circuits that make it easy for you to feel bad about being in the one-down position and bad about being in the one-up position. You could spend your whole life longing for the position you're not in. Or you could build up the circuits that find the good in what you have:

- When you're in the subordinate position, notice the advantages. Someone else is in the "hot seat." You're not responsible for protecting others, and you don't have to worry about defending your position.
- When you're in the dominant position, enjoy the moments of respect and choice instead of being overwhelmed by the pressure, because those moments will end.

For forty-five days, notice your status frustrations and remind yourself of the hidden advantages of wherever you are. Your status will always be going up and down in small ways. Your mammal brain will always keep track of it, as much as you wish it wouldn't. If you fret over your position, the fretting will never end. You can focus on the positives instead. Once you create this thought habit, you will always have a way to make peace with your mammal brain.

Notice Your Influence

Many people try to raise their status by looking for the bad in others. They feel good about themselves in comparison, but they pay a high price for this serotonin boost. It surrounds them with bad will. You can make a small change that stimulates your serotonin without the harmful side effect. Simply enjoy your influence on others. Without criticizing or controlling, you can notice when others mirror your good example. Don't expect credit or even a thank you. Just quietly enjoy.

This may sound arrogant, but every mammal brain longs for social significance. Everyone wants to have an impact on the world and fears dying without a trace. If you don't meet the need in healthy ways, you will be tempted to meet it in ways that hurt. Some people cause harm intentionally just to feel their impact. There is an alternative: Value the impact you already have.

Right this minute, people may be respecting you behind your back. If your antennae are busy looking for disrespect, you won't know it. People may be secretly admiring you, and instead of enjoying it, you may be anticipating criticism from them. If so, you're wasting that potential serotonin boost.

Stop once a day to appreciate your good effect on others. Don't call attention to it or say "I told you so." Simply look for your subtle influence and feel satisfied. If you do this for forty-five days, you will feel satisfied by your ability to influence the world and you will feel less frustrated by other people's flaws and neglect. You will have a mental pathway to feel good about your social importance.

Parents often bemoan their lack of influence over their children. If they knew how much they really do influence their kids in the long run, they would pay more attention to the example they set.

Make Peace with Something You Can't Control

Your brain looks for things you can control and feels good when you're in charge. But our control is often limited and unpredictable, so frustration percolates. You can learn to feel comfortable with your limited control. That doesn't mean being out of control or giving up. It means feeling safe when you're not in charge.

To build this new circuit, notice your usual strategy for feeling "on top of things," and do the opposite. For example, if you are a person who tries to bake the perfect soufflé, spend forty-five days cooking without recipes. Conversely, if you are a person who likes to just throw things into a pot, spend forty-five days following recipes.

If you are a person who likes everything neat, let junk pile up for six weeks. But if you are a person who hates order and loves chaos, put things away as soon as you use them for six weeks.

Color outside the lines if that's new for you, but if you already pride yourself on that, courageously stay inside the lines. It might feel awful on Day One, but forty-four days later it will feel curiously safe.

Getting rid of the clock is a great way to experiment with control, because you can't control time. We all have habits for managing the harsh reality of time. For some it's chronic lateness and for others it's constant clock-checking. You may think you can't change your relationship with time, but here are three great ways to ignore the clock and make friends with the passage of time:

1. Start an activity without having an exact time you need to stop. Finish the activity without ever checking the clock the whole time. It's over when you feel like it's over.
2. Set aside a time each day to spend with no plan.
3. Designate a day you can wake up without looking at the clock and continue through your day with no time-checking.

No matter how busy you are, you can find a way to relax your efforts to control time. You may be surprised at the bad feelings that come up, despite your abiding wish to escape time pressure. The bad feelings won't kill you, however, and accepting them helps you accept the harsh realities of time.

Your mammal brain feels good about things it can control. Some people break traffic laws to enjoy a sense of control, while others feel their power by scolding those who break traffic laws. Whatever gives you a sense of power won't work all the time, however. You will end up feeling weak and unimportant some of the time. That triggers cortisol, but you can learn to feel safe when you are not in control.

For forty-five days, give up control instead of trying to control the world in your accustomed ways. Don't quit your day job to beg with a rice bowl. Just stop checking the weather report, buying lottery tickets, and expecting the world to work according to your rules. Choose one habit you have for feeling in control, and do without it. If you can't give up your control ritual completely, commit to giving it up for a certain time each day. You will learn to feel safe in the world despite your inability to control it.

EXERCISE: WHAT ARE YOUR NEW SEROTONIN STRATEGIES?

Remodeling projects that can work for me:

Express pride in what I've done

_____

_____

_____

Enjoy my social position in each moment

_____

_____

_____

Notice my influence

_____

_____

_____

Make peace with something I can't control

_____

_____

_____

The Challenges of Establishing a Habit

If you were planning a trip to the Amazon, you'd have to choose between interesting places far from paved roads and destinations that are easily accessible. The exotic locales would entice you, but when you saw what it took to get there, you might gravitate toward the beaten path.

It's the same with your jungle of neurons. New goals sound great, but once you start slogging toward them, well-paved neural highways may tempt you. You can build a new highway if you slog for forty-five days. Exciting destinations will become accessible, so your old roads will be less tempting.

To establish a new trail through your jungle of neurons, you must repeat a new behavior every day. Otherwise, the undergrowth will return and your next pass will be just as hard as the first. Spark your new trail each day whether or not you feel like it, and you will eventually pass it with ease. You may not get the highs of your old happy habit, but you will learn to feel good without artificial highs and their inevitable side effects. You will be so pleased with your new habit that you will want to build another, and another.

It bears repeating that you will not be happy on Day One. Maintain realistic expectations. Nibbling on carrot sticks will not feel as good as licking an ice cream cone on Day One, and it may not seem that this could change with repetition. Doing homework will not feel as good as watching a movie on Day One, and it's hard to imagine that changing either. Stick to your plan and you will connect carrot sticks or studying to your happy chemicals. You can feel good when you do what's good for you.

Linking the Past and the Future

I stumbled on the power of repetition when I noticed that certain music made me happy. I don't mean music I actually like. I don't mean memories-of-the-beach music. I mean music that was forced on me by accidents of experience. When I was young, my ears were often filled with sounds chosen by my brother, my father, my boss at work, and the cafeteria I ate in. Today, when one of these songs reaches my ears, I feel strangely happy, even though I didn't like it at the time. This mystified me until I read a book called *Flow*, by Mihaly Csikszentmihalyi. It explained that music gives pleasure because your mind keeps predicting what comes next. Each correct prediction triggers dopamine. You can't make good predictions for unfamiliar music, so you don't get the dopamine. But when music is too familiar, something strange happens. You don't get the dopamine either because your brain predicts it effortlessly. To make you happy, music must be at the sweet spot of novelty and familiarity.

The music that makes you happy today will eventually fail to make you happy, because it will become too familiar. At the same time, music that doesn't make you happy today can make you happy in the future. If you want to stay happy, it seems you have to expose yourself to unfamiliar music now, so it will be in the sweet spot by the time you've worn out your old pleasures. This was a revelation to me. It explains why happiness is elusive despite our best efforts. And it shows how the counterintuitive choice to repeat things we don't already like can bring great rewards. We talk about "good music" and "bad music" as if the quality is inherent in the music. We overlook the power of the circuits we bring to that music. Your pleasures are shaped by circuits you built without knowing it. It's natural to presume the things you like are somehow special and the things you don't like are somehow lacking. But you can learn to shape your circuits in ways that expand good feelings.

Overcome Initial Unpleasantness

The first step is a willingness to do things that don't feel good at first. This is difficult because your brain usually trusts its own reactions. You don't usually listen to music you dislike on the assumption that you'll grow to like it. You don't befriend a person you dislike or join an activity you're bad at on the assumption that something will change. It's natural to trust your current likes and dislikes. But now you know that they're based on accidents of experience rather than complete information. Your accidental circuits cause the threatened feeling you get when you depart from the road you know. If you avoid the threatened feeling by sticking to the old road, you miss out on a universe of potential happiness. You can learn to enjoy the challenge of embarking on a new road.

Make a Commitment to One Pathway at First

With so many choices and so many neurons, you can build a lot of new pathways to your happy chemicals. But you only have a limited amount of time and energy. If you spread it everywhere, a new road may not get built. So choose one remodeling project to start with. Commit to repeating it for forty-five days whether or not you feel like it. If you miss a day, start over with Day One.

Commitments to yourself can be difficult to enforce. For example, I made the commitment to bring reusable bags with me when I buy food, but I kept forgetting them. So I added the commitment to go back to my car and get them if I forgot. The next time I found myself at the supermarket without the bags, I thought "I'm too busy to go back to the car." Then I realized that I will always be busy, and I am a powerless person if I can't even honor a commitment to myself. So I went back to the car to get the bags, and I never forgot them again because I didn't want to waste time going back to my car.

You will not want to waste time starting over with Day One. You will want to honor your commitments to yourself and thus enjoy a new happy habit. The following chapters lead you through a series of commitments to your first remodeling project. After that, you will love your new power over your brain, and find many ways to use it.

7 | YOUR ACTION PLAN

Formulate a Plan That Works for You

We've all heard that a long journey begins with the first step, but we all know it's more complicated. Before the first step, you have to choose the right course so you step in the right direction. After the first step, you know how deep the mud is but you have to find the will to take the next step anyway. To complete forty-five steps, you need an action plan you believe in. You need to choose the first new happy habit you want to build, the date you will start, and the tools that will ease your steps. This chapter and those following will help you commit to those choices.

EXERCISE: TIMELINE FOR YOUR COMMITMENT TO SELF

Finish this chapter on choosing a new habit by (date)

_____

Finish next chapter on choosing happiness over unhappiness by (date) _____

Finish final chapter on tools by (date)

_____

How to Overcome the Inevitable Internal Conflicts You Will Face

When you embark on a plan to stimulate one happy chemical, you can see how it might undermine another happy chemical. If you seek more serotonin, for example, you may see a threat to your oxytocin. And if you seek more oxytocin, it may feel like a setback for your serotonin. When you seek dopamine in one way, you have less energy to seek it another way. And your cortisol may be triggered by any and every kind of seeking. You may wish for a perfect plan before you take your first step, but perfect never comes. You will have to make tradeoffs on your way to a new happy habit.

Fortunately, our brain evolved to make tradeoffs:

- A dog can only dig for a bone by passing up the chance to dig in another spot.
- An elephant has to choose in every moment between following her nose and following her herd.
- A lion chooses between the fear of hunting alone and the fear of hunting with mates who hog the food.

Like those animals, you will always be choosing among imperfect options. If you focus on drawbacks and imperfections, it's hard to commit. Here's a close look at the inevitable tradeoffs of life. Think them through now and you will approach your new habit with confidence.

Short Run vs. Long Run

We constantly weigh immediate rewards against rewards we expect in the future. If you decide to smoke, you are trading off future rewards for a present reward. If you decide to party, you are choosing one set of rewards, and if you decide not to party, you get a different set. We cannot predict these rewards perfectly, but better predictions bring better rewards.

To make good predictions, you have to choose good information. But we tend to rely on the information-filtering habits built into our circuits by accident. If you change your information-filtering habits, you will suddenly make new tradeoffs between short- and long-term rewards. For example, if you think you are a powerless victim of powerful forces, you will overlook the power of your own choices. Once you believe that your actions have consequences, you will find the information you need about the consequences. Then you will make more rewarding tradeoffs between the long and short run.

Known vs. Unknown

We are always trading off the safety of the known against the promise of the unknown. Sometimes we stick with the known until we find an alternative that feels like a sure thing, and sometimes we risk an alternative before it's fully baked. Once you choose, you see the drawbacks of your choice up close, but you never know how the other option would have turned out. So it's easy to end up frustrated about your own choices.

Instead, you can learn to honor your decision-making ability. Uncertainty is inevitable, so there's no use judging yourself against idealized optimums. I am not saying you should defend your decisions to the point of refusing to learn from them. But if you only attack your decisions, you will never make a choice unless there's absolute certainty. Celebrate your ability to live with uncertainty and you will broaden your options.

Individual vs. Group

The protection of a group feels good, but striking out on your own feels good too. It would be nice to have both, but that's not a realistic expectation. Painful choices are everywhere and we often make them worse by focusing on what we're missing. You miss your independence when you're in a group, and you miss the safety of the group when you follow your individual impulses. Unhappy chemicals surge when you focus on the down side of each option. You could focus on the benefits you are currently enjoying instead—enjoy the group when it's group time and enjoy your individuality when you're alone.

Appreciating what you have is difficult to do because the mind naturally seeks what it doesn't have. It's natural to feel the squeeze on your personal interests while you have group support. And when you go your own way, it's natural to worry about the loss of social ties. We want to have it all, but this tradeoff is part of being human. Instead of expecting it to go away, pride yourself on your ability to manage it.

Free Will vs. Dependency

If you were an animal in a zoo, you might envy wild animals and try to break free. But if you were a wild animal, you might break *into* the zoo to enjoy food that comes effortlessly. At the zoo where I volunteer, animals often break in, and rarely break out. Meeting your own needs often feels like a burden, but when you are dependent on others to meet your needs for you, you miss out on happy chemicals, because they are stimulated by the act of meeting your own needs.

A wild animal lives with great stress as it struggles to fill its belly, compete for mates, and protect its offspring from predators. Though we like to imagine a pristine state of nature, meeting your needs is stressful. Yet this is the job our brain evolved for, and escaping the burden does not make it happy. You may long to be taken care of, but if you actually escaped the burden of meeting your own needs, you would find yourself surprisingly unhappy. You might end up filling your life with stress about the inadequacy of what's given to you. You might feel trapped in rage at your caretakers while fearing to leave them and return to a life of meeting your own needs.

Choice is so frustrating that a person sometimes opts to live in a "zoo," meaning, they want to be protected and led. When they feel bad, they don't know why, so they blame the zookeeper for failing to meet their needs adequately. They resent anyone they believe to have power over them, and end up with perpetual hostility toward their providers and leaders. They enjoy a sense of personal power by putting down those they perceive as more powerful. But this habit never really makes up for the personal power you lose when you make others responsible for meeting your needs. Find the joy of meeting your own needs instead. You can celebrate your freedom to choose your steps instead of experiencing them as a burden.

EXERCISE: WHAT ARE YOUR TRADEOFFS?

There is no perfect path to happiness. You will always have to navigate tradeoffs as you build new pathways. Write down the choices you will face as you attempt to build your first new circuit:

Short run vs. long run

_____

_____

_____

_____

Known vs. unknown

_____

_____

_____

_____

Individual vs. group

_____

_____

_____

_____

Free will vs. dependency

_____

_____

_____

_____

The Burden of Choice

There is no set path to happy chemicals. There is only a constant string of decisions to risk something in the expectation of gaining something else.

Talking about "good decisions" and "bad decisions" creates the impression that there is an optimal path. If you believe in a right path, you compare your life to an idealized image that does not exist. That can leave you focused on disappointments and believing you're on the wrong path, even in the midst of a good life. Instead, you can accept the fact that you will always have ups and downs because your brain is designed to continually seek rewards and avoid pain.

If you have two good choices, you can get so caught up in regretting the choice you gave up that you skim over the happiness you have and end up with a lot of cortisol. Choice is so challenging that people are sometimes tempted to shift the burden of choice onto others. This strategy doesn't relieve the cortisol of endlessly lamenting what you don't have, but it relieves your frustration with yourself by blaming it on others.

There is an alternative. You can think of life as a series of tradeoffs rather than an optimization function with one correct solution. Tough calls are inevitable, but you are the best judge of the fine-tuned tradeoffs of your own life.

Your brain will never stop trying to promote your survival. It takes what you have for granted and looks for ways to get more—more rewards (dopamine), more physical security (endorphin), more social support (oxytocin), more respect (serotonin). Seeking more is risky. Your brain is constantly deciding whether it's worth giving up some of this to get more of that. Once you decide, you may not get the outcome you expected. The frustration may tempt you to leave the hard calls to someone else, but you will end up with more happy chemicals if you carry your own burden of choice.

EXERCISE: WHICH NEW HABIT DO I CHOOSE?

I will retrain my brain to build a new happy habit. The new behavior or thought habit I will build is

_____

_____

_____

I will repeat it every day for forty-five days whether or not I feel like it, and start over with Day One if I miss a day. As I take the new steps, I may be stepping away from something else, but I can manage the tradeoffs on the trail to a new reward.

8 | OVER-COMING OBSTACLES TO HAPPINESS

Why Stick with Unhappiness?

If you could be happy in forty-five days with just a few minutes of effort per day, why wouldn't you? This chapter explains what is going on in your brain when you experience some common rationales for sticking with unhappy habits. You will probably recognize these reasons and the vicious cycles they lead to. Once you notice your own way of choosing unhappiness, you can make alternate choices that will lead you to happiness.

Reason #1: "I Can't Lower My Standards"

"Why should I be happy with small things," you may ask. "I have high aspirations." It's natural to assume big things will make you happy since we've all felt the big spurt of a big achievement. But big achievers are not necessarily happy. This is so hard to believe that tabloid news does a public service by constantly reminding us. Shunning big achievements does not guarantee happiness either, alas. Nothing guarantees it. You can help it along, however, by focusing on ways to meet your needs.

In today's culture, people claim their high standards are for the sake of others. They insist they cannot be happy until they "save the world." People even assert that it's unethical to be happy as long as one person is suffering, or even one animal. But the world has always been full of suffering. Is it unethical for anyone in human history to have ever been happy? No. This is just the verbal brain's effort to explain the mammal brain's quirky quest for happy chemicals. If you refuse to accept your inner mammal's urge for more, you construct lofty-sounding explanations for your frustrations. But blaming your unhappiness on higher ethics does not bring you neurochemical peace.

You may have the illusion that happiness is just handed to a lucky few, while others are wrongly deprived of it. You may think you must earn happiness by suffering. This often works for a moment, as your sense of superiority triggers serotonin and the perceived trust triggers oxytocin. This may tempt you to suffer more to enjoy another squirt of happy chemicals. Suffering can give you a sense of importance, and shared suffering helps build social bonds. But the good feelings soon pass, and it seems like you must suffer to stimulate more. The vicious cycle is obvious. You can't let go of suffering because you fear losing what happiness you have. You don't realize that suffering is just a circuit your mammal brain built because it was rewarded in your past. You might even tell yourself that happiness would make you one of the bad guys who steals it from others.

> **FOCUS ON YOURSELF**
> You cannot make yourself responsible for other people's suffering, and you cannot make other people responsible for your suffering. Other people get to manage their happy chemicals with the circuits they've got, and you get to manage your happy chemicals with the circuits you've got.

You get frustrated while waiting for the world to meet your high standards, and you might relieve it by engaging in a bad habit. You justify the bad habit by pointing to the flaws of the world. For example, you may catch yourself thinking: "With the state of the world as it is, why shouldn't I drink/take drugs/eat junk food/have affairs/borrow and spend/rage at people?" As the bad habit becomes the focus of your life, you keep finding more ways to suffer to keep justifying your indulgence in the habit. This vicious cycle is a common by-product of the "high standards" mentality.

If you take an idealized view of happiness, it will always be out of reach. But you are free to be happy with small things instead of waiting for the world to meet your idealized requirements.

Well-intentioned people often choose suffering without realizing it. Teachers and parents often choose suffering for their students by encouraging unrealistic expectations. If you try to motivate a class with the idea of becoming president or winning the Olympics, most of the students in the class will end up frustrated. It's more helpful to teach students that everyone, even presidents and Olympic medalists, experience neurochemical ups and downs that they must learn to manage. Students are better off learning skills that will meet their needs, like literacy, math, and self-management habits, than learning grandiose aspirations. Focusing on skills is not "lowering standards."

"High standards" sound nice, but it can be an excuse for living with bitterness and resentment while you're waiting for some abstract ideal. High standards can actually lead to low standards if you exclude a realistic middle ground. Meeting your own survival needs is the standard your brain evolved for, so that is what makes you feel good.

Reason #2: "I Shouldn't Have to Do This"

You may be thinking, "Other people get to be happy without repeating things for forty-five days. Why should I have to?"

Maybe you think you've done more than enough already and it's time for the rest of the world to do its part. Maybe you think you are owed something, so why should you "let the jerks off the hook" by making yourself happy. You will be happy when "the jerks" do what you think is "the right thing."

Many people think settling a score with those who have shortchanged them is the path to happiness. Once you look at life this way, you will easily find evidence that you have been wronged and you will easily find company to share your view. Unfortunately, this strategy is likely to distract you from taking steps that would actually bring happiness.

I've often heard my students say it's unfair they have to work hard at coursework while someone else seems to "get it" effortlessly. I hear dieters say it's unfair that others stay thin effortlessly. If you think happiness comes effortlessly to others, you might decide that it's unfair for you to have to work at it. If you feel wronged by life, you may give yourself permission to have another cookie, another drink, another pill, or another sulk. After all you've been through, why deprive yourself anymore? This is a vicious cycle. You keep feeling wronged in order to enjoy more of your favorite consolation prize.

It's easy to believe that others are luckier than you in the happy-circuit department. We mammals naturally compare ourselves to others. But we never really know the inside story about other people's lives. Even if you did, it wouldn't make you happy. Taking inventory for others diverts you from doing what it takes to trigger your own happy chemicals.

If you are always searching for wrongs, you don't notice what's right, even if you stumble on it. And yet, this mindset is curiously popular. You wire it in when you are young, pleasing teachers with essays on the awful state of the world, and mirroring parents who feel deprived themselves.

Some people have no experience making themselves happy because they grew up in a world in which others took responsibility for their happiness. Some parents live to please their children and never please themselves. Their children learn to expect others to please them, and another generation learns to take unhappiness as a sign that others messed up instead of learning to please themselves.

Blaming others for your unhappiness is a habit that's hard to give up because of the immediate rewards:

- You feel important when you battle perceived injustice (serotonin).
- You feel connected with others who feel similarly deprived (oxytocin).
- You feel excitement when you seek and find evidence that your fair share of happiness was wrongfully denied (dopamine).
- You may even trigger endorphin by welcoming physical pain into your life as evidence of your deprivation.
- You keep building the circuit for seeking happiness by feeling wronged.

A stopped clock is right twice a day, so if you look for evidence that your share of happiness was mistakenly distributed to the undeserving, you will certainly find it. But it will only make you happy for a moment, and then you will need to find more such evidence. You don't do what it takes to create your own happiness as long as you believe it is doled out by "them."

If you decide to build new happy circuits, you might be the happiest person you know six weeks from now. But you won't commit if you believe you shouldn't have to. If you think others are getting it for free, you end up shortchanging yourself.

Reason #3: "It's Selfish to Focus on Your Own Happiness"

Many people take a zero-sum view of happiness. Whether consciously or unconsciously, they think one person's happiness takes away from others. When my mother was scrubbing the floor in an angry rage, she thought she would be happy if I were doing the scrubbing. So I got on my knees and scrubbed, preferring that to being indicted for "selfishness." But it did not make my mother happy. This was a huge lesson. I used to feel obliged to join in her misery, like the captain who must go down with a sinking ship. But I learned that I was not the captain of her ship. I could only be the captain of my own.

Looking back, I see that my mother wanted company. She didn't know how to stop scrubbing, so she wanted company in her prison. She was not forced to scrub by "our society." It's a habit she built long ago, when it seemed to promote survival. I kept trying to make her happy, but nothing worked. If I focused on making myself happy instead, she would condemn me for selfishness, but I decided that was better than being miserable.

When you stimulate your own happy chemicals, you are not depriving others of them. Each adult is free to make his own calls in pursuit of happiness—as long as he takes responsibility for their side effects and avoids making himself happy at the expense of children. You are not obligated to subordinate your happiness to other adults. And others are not obligated to subordinate their happiness to you. Of course, you will want to cooperate in pursuit of mutual goals, but you get to define when and how you cooperate, and live with the consequences. If someone insists you must subordinate your survival needs to theirs, you don't have to agree. And if you expect others to subordinate their needs to yours, you need a new plan.

You have surely heard that happiness comes from unselfishly devoting yourself to others. It sounds nice, but your brain is motivated by the expectation of rewards. If you devote yourself to others, you are expecting a reward from doing that, and if the reward doesn't come, you feel bad. You can end up feeling bad a lot, and you won't even know why if you don't acknowledge your expectations of reward. You can end up adding bitterness to the world even as you intended to add good. So you could actually help the world by being real about your natural "selfish" urges. Many people refuse to do this, so the world is still full of bitter people raging at the world for its selfishness while believing in their own unselfishness.

> **MODEL "FEELING GOOD" FOR OTHERS**
> If you give yourself permission to feel good, it can actually help others. It can trigger their mirror neurons and spark their happiness. But you cannot make yourself feel good just for the sake of others. Your brain doesn't work that way; it focuses on you. You must step toward your needs to stimulate your happy chemicals.

The confusion is rooted in the fact that rescuing others indeed stimulates happy chemicals:

- Serotonin flows when your rescuing gets respect.
- Oxytocin flows when you join forces with others.
- Dopamine flows when you set goals and accomplish them.

But these spurts are soon over and you need to rescue again to feel good. Many rescuers persist when they do more harm than good. Your efforts to save others may have harmful consequences that you ignore because you need the selfish rewards of being a rescuer. You can do more good for the world by finding new paths to happiness.

Every brain builds a sense of its own well-being that's separate from others. This is the job the brain evolved to do. Being alone with your neurochemistry can be uncomfortable, and a person might avoid this discomfort by enmeshing themselves in the neurochemistry of others. Sometimes your enmeshment gets rewarded, and that wires you to expect more good feeling from more enmeshment. Escaping into the experiences of others can therefore become a habit. You may think you will always be happy by taking charge of other people's happiness or by expecting others to take charge of yours. But your brain is always keeping track of what's good for *you*. If your happy chemicals are not flowing, only you can take the steps to trigger them.

If you decide to be happy, you may feel conspicuous and out of step among those who decide differently. You may fear being called selfish, and you might even feign suffering to avoid it. The problem is real because social bonds are often built on shared suffering. Many people focus on the suffering of children, or animals, or the planet. Of course, it's good to help children, animals, and the planet, but much of this shared suffering does not actually help. It's just an effort to meet selfish needs. If you don't join in the shared suffering, people may indeed sneer at you. But in the past, people tortured and executed you if you didn't join the shared belief system; so when I get sneered at for not joining in an unhappy thought habit, I'm just grateful that sneering is such a small penalty.

It's reasonable to feel bad about the suffering of others and to help where you can. But your brain is designed to focus on *your* well-being. Acknowledging your needs does not mean you are judging or abandoning others. You are respecting others as individuals responsible for their own needs. You are securing your own oxygen mask first, as they tell you on an airplane. If you put your happiness in other people's hands, a vicious cycle is the likely result. Taking the reins of your own life is your only real choice. You cannot control the reins for other lives or expect others to manage yours.

Reason #4: "I Want to Be Prepared for the Worst"

Will you lose your edge if you let yourself be happy? Does happiness lower your guard and disadvantage you when things go wrong? Does unhappiness make you more apt to survive?

No. It's natural to scan for potential threats, but focusing on familiar threats does not protect you from new threats. So you actually make yourself safer when you stay open to new and unexpected information about the world. Preparing for the kind of threat you've already experienced is just a habit that you could replace with a new habit.

You may not notice that you are scanning for familiar threats. You may intend to be open to the good in the world. But when it reaches your eyes and ears, you may ignore it, because your bandwidth is quickly spent on information that fits your past rewards and pain. You have to intentionally shift your focus away from them to notice the fainter signals of new threats and opportunities. But this shift can feel like a survival threat because your brain equates past rewards and pain with survival. This is why people tend to stay focused on old threats.

You may feel like stuff is hitting the fan while you're building those new circuits. That's your old superhighways lighting up. Stay focused on good things instead of those crisis-mentality fireworks and you will have a new superhighway in forty-five days. You will see more in the world than potential calamity. You may be alone in that world if everyone you know is distracted by disaster preparedness, but you have the power to choose that anyway.

We all have a brain that releases happy chemicals in short spurts, so we all have to live with the dips that come at the end of a spurt. When a dip happens, it's easy to focus on danger signals, release unhappy chemicals, start preparing, and restart the cycle. It's easy to expect a cataclysm. You can end this vicious cycle in one instant, just by shifting your attention elsewhere. It may feel awful at first, as you resist the urge to "do something" while your social allies are in crisis mode. But you will survive that instant, and you will courageously refuse to contemplate disaster for the next instant, and the next. Eventually, you will create a gap big enough to fill with positive expectations. A happy circuit will grow big enough to compete for your attention.

> **CONSIDER THIS**
> When things do go wrong, ask yourself whether you could have prevented it by being unhappy.

Your cortex is skilled at finding the information it looks for. If you don't look for the good in the world, it will easily escape your attention. When you start looking for the good, it can feel like you're frittering your attention and taking your eye off the ball. But bad things are curiously unpredictable, so a siege mentality just wears you out. Happiness builds a cushion that prepares you for bumpy roads better than unhappiness.

Reason #5: "I Won't Be Able to Do This"

What if you try to build a new circuit and fail? It's a horrible thought, and you may avoid it by refusing to try.

Forty-five days is a long time to invest if you expect to fail. No one wants to spend forty-five days worried about blowing it. Failure is easy to imagine, because your brain has already greased those skids. If a new habit were easy to imagine, you'd already be doing it. So the challenge is to start without a clear conception of the finish.

The way to do that is to focus on your next step. You can expect that one step to succeed, even if you've failed in the past. Expecting success doesn't mean lying to yourself and others; it means being honest about the trial and error nature of success.

Disappointment is always possible, but a next step is always possible too. If you refuse to take a step until you're sure of being right, you limit yourself significantly. Instead, you can accept being wrong as a step on a path that isn't perfectly predictable. Error is not a sign of incompetence; it's a sign that you are facing an unknown that must be explored before it can be mastered.

Failure triggers circuits etched by past failures, which amplifies the electricity of small disappointments. Day One of your circuit-building program can unleash the ghosts of everything you've ever done wrong, which makes Day Two feel like a huge step. But if you give up on Day Two, your failure circuit is strengthened. To stop this vicious cycle, you must take the step you committed to even when it feels bad. Tell yourself "I did it!" even if the only thing you did was thinking "I did it!" while feeling like you didn't. This may feel fake at first, but if you persist, your success circuit will start to feel as true as your failure circuit.

Of course, you don't want to be a deluded person who pats himself on the back for no reason . . . but you may already be kicking yourself for no reason. Accidents of past experience will define you until you shape new experiences into new circuits. With each step, you are either building a new circuit or strengthening an old circuit.

Reason #6: "Who Can Be Happy in Such a Flawed Society?"

My college professors taught me to blame "the system" for human misery. I got praise if I linked human problems to the flaws of "our society." Questioning that presumption brought harsh disdain, I learned. I didn't want to be condemned as a person who "doesn't get it," so I "got it." I even became a college professor and taught a new generation to blame their frustrations on "our society." If I was not convinced that tearing down the system would make everyone happy, I kept my mouth shut.

But I encountered many realities that did not fit the model—biological, historical, and personal realities—and I grew in my ability to tolerate life outside the popular consensus. So I faced the fact that human nature is more complicated than the lyrics to a 1960s folk song.

For example, I learned that the frustrations we blame on our system are widespread in other cultures and other times. Often they're much worse in those other times and places, but not publicly acknowledged. Yet mentioning the unhappiness of other cultures or periods can easily get you shunned by thought leaders ostensibly concerned with truth.

KNOWLEDGE IS POWER

When your happy chemicals droop, it feels like something is wrong with the world. It helps to know that your happy chemicals are meant to go up and down so you can focus on your next step toward happy chemicals instead of on the flaws of the world.

You can imagine a better world that will make you happy all the time—in fact, just thinking about your better world stimulates your happy chemicals. You get a bigger boost when you imagine yourself fixing the flaws of today's world, and an even bigger boost when you bond with others who share your perceived threat. These chemicals pave a circuit that keeps you focused on a world that does not exist—a world that would not, in fact, bring constant happiness if it suddenly appeared. You feed the dream by hating your reality. It's a vicious cycle because you have to focus on the bad in the world to maintain your membership in the club.

"The personal is political" was a popular slogan when I was young. Early feminists promoted the idea that personal problems are caused by political failures, and thus must be solved by political action. I was surrounded by this world view for most of my life. But I learned from experience that the political is personal. The ups and downs of our personal lives are so frustrating that we long to believe the political system can fix them for us.

When you blame your frustrations on abstract institutions, it helps you avoid blaming real people you know in person. It feels good in the short run to avoid conflict with friends and family. But you never work things out with flesh-and-blood people when your attention is focused on imagined conflict with "the man."

I grew up watching extreme unhappiness and wanted to do everything possible to make sure my kids did not grow up in that way. So as much as I would rather have blamed my problems on "our society" like everyone around me, I did not want to overlook other obvious causes of unhappiness. So I took the risk of connecting the dots, even if it meant getting separated from the herd. I saw that primates do not always get along, and if political anger is your primary tool for working through these frictions, you get disappointed. People who say society has to change before they can meet their needs end up disappointed. I wanted my kids to manage their own neurochemical ups and downs instead of expecting the system to do it for them. And if I wanted my kids to do that, I needed to build that skill myself.

So I faced the inevitability of human frustration. Each brain sees itself as the center of the world, though it is just 1 of 7 billion. Each brain panics at the thought of lethal threats, yet must live with the knowledge that it will die someday and the world will spin on anyway. These harsh realities will always trigger unhappy chemicals. No social system can protect you from them. Blaming bad feelings on the system and demanding a fix from the system can distract you from building the essential skill of managing your neurochemical ups and downs. If you externalize your dips by blaming them on forces outside yourself, you don't learn to make peace with your own internal system. Each brain is free to choose peace, or to choose blame.

I frequently encounter people who choose blame. They can't stop eating junk food until "our society stops eating junk food." They can't stop feeling shame until "our society stops shaming you." They can't stop worrying about the future until "our society addresses the future." They can't feel well because "our society is sick." They believe they cannot change unless everyone else changes first. If you put "our society" in charge of your brain, you make yourself powerless. When you put yourself in charge of your own happiness, you have power.

The system-failure view of life is like a drug: easy to start and hard to stop. You may start because teachers and professors praise your work when you criticize "the system," and you realize you can get "As" without doing the reading if you stick to that pattern. You realize that a social group will accept you if you blame their shared frustrations on the system. You continue this thought habit to avoid damaging the career and personal relationships you've nurtured for years. They may call you "smug" if you question the shared hostility toward "the system." They may call you "privileged" if you take responsibility for your own happiness. They may even start blaming their unhappiness on you. But you still have a choice. You can repeat the rallying cries of starving serfs from past centuries, or you can accept your own mammalian urges and be glad you have that choice.

When you stop believing that the system can make you happy, you are stuck with the awful prospect of doing it yourself. It's much easier to tussle with philosophical abstractions than to deal with actual people who get on your nerves. Fixing the system seems to be more fun and more righteous than fixing yourself. But when you understand your inner mammal, you realize that nothing is wrong with you. You are simply a mammal among mammals.

Of course, you keep tripping over the fact that your time on earth is limited and you are not the center of the world. Your brain cries out "do something!" One thing you can do is to join with others who feel the same way and "demand that your voice be heard." But when you expect public institutions to satisfy that deep human longing to be heard, you get disappointed. The "do something" feeling continues because your mortality still weighs on you. These feelings are so hard to manage that many people externalize them with thoughts of an apocalypse of one variety or another. You can free yourself from such thoughts by understanding your own brain.

Reason #7: "I'll Be Happy When . . ."

It's natural to think you'll be happy when you reach some particular benchmark. I'll be happy when I can finish a triathlon, or get my grandchildren into a good school, or stop AIDS. But goals are double-edged swords. They stimulate happy chemicals with each step closer, but they stimulate unhappy chemicals with each obstacle. If you respond to each dip by rushing toward your goal, you can end up in a vicious cycle. You are better off having a variety of tools to manage your happy chemicals.

Approaching a goal feels good because your brain has connected it to survival. Of course, you know you can survive without winning the Executive Bonus Pool or the Stand-Up Comedy Olympics, but it feels different once your cortisol is triggered. You can distract yourself from that do-something feeling by focusing more intently on your goal. You may tell yourself you can't stop until you "get a break" or "get it right." You can imagine how good it will feel.

But if you do reach that important milestone, the feeling doesn't last. All too soon, your cortisol is triggered in one way or another. You respond in the only way you know how: zooming in on another goal.

People often say they are forced to do this by "our society." They don't see how they are choosing it, even though they can see that in others. The urge to "make something of yourself" is natural. It's much older than our society, and it's much deeper than the urge for money or power. Your brain wants to leave a legacy and you only have a limited amount of time to do that. Our sense of urgency is real. Advancing your legacy is a good tool for managing these feelings, but it's not enough. We need many tools to manage our feelings of urgency because they are so powerful. If you only have one path to your happy chemicals, a bad loop results.

Single-minded pursuit of a goal makes everything else seem like an obstacle. Other people, your physical body, and even rules and laws can seem like obstacles. Life feels like an escalator and if it's not moving up, you think it's broken down. You can free yourself from an escalator if you are willing to do something different for forty-five days. Do not simply replace one goal with another. Instead, build the habit of having multiple sources of satisfaction. Your new circuits cannot trigger happy chemicals every minute, but they can help you manage the cortisol blast you feel when you ease off your goal.

It's hard to avoid the escalator view of happiness if you watch the news. Following the news fills your circuits with people who are getting a lot of attention. Your mirror neurons take it in, and give you the sense that you would be happy all the time if you were among their elite circle. Of course, you would not be happy all the time if you raised your social dominance, but you may never get into a position where you find that out. You could spend your whole life believing you'd be happy if only you were a rung higher on your imagined ladder.

The alternative is to make peace with your mammalian status urge. Don't hate that urge, because you will end up hating yourself and everyone else. Just accept it and appreciate your ability to invest your energy in different ways.

> **EXERCISE: FINDING YOUR OBSTACLES AND ELIMINATING THEM**
>
> Are you letting these thoughts deprive you of happiness? How?
>
> I can't lower my standards.
>
> I shouldn't have to do this.
>
> It's selfish to focus on your own happiness.
>
> I want to be prepared for the worst.
>
> I won't be able to do this.
>
> Who can be happy in such a flawed society?
>
> I'll be happy when . . .

Choose Happiness

You are master of the quirky neural network built by your life experience. You get to decide which thoughts and behaviors are good for you. When your unhappy chemicals flow, you have the power to send your electricity in a new direction. That creates space for a new thought to grow. At first it will just be a trickle of electricity, but a new happy habit will build if you persist. Choose that new habit wisely.

EXERCISE: WHAT IS YOUR START DATE?

Starting on (date)

_____

I will repeat my chosen thought habit or behavior every day for forty-five days. I will make the energy available whether it feels like a walk in the park or a trudge through the mud. If I miss a day, I will start over with Day One until I reach forty-five.

9 | RELY ON TOOLS THAT ARE ALWAYS WITH YOU

Circuit Training for Your Brain

Your brain is equipped with many circuit-building tools. You can rely on these built-in tools when the going gets tough. When you feel like something is wrong even though you know you're doing right, these tools are with you. Following are descriptions of the trail-blazing tools that will help you stay on your new path until it gets established. Think of ways you can commit to them when you're tempted by the comfort of your old path.

Mirror

Mirror people who already have the habits you want. Find someone with a habit you'd like to create, and watch them. Your mirror neurons will light up and spark your circuits. This is a great way to overcome the inertia of those virgin neurons.

Modeling others can be awkward, but the world is full of people who have the behavior you need. Maybe they'd love to show you. If not, you can mirror without telling them. They may not even be consciously aware of their habit anyway.

The person you are mirroring may surprise you by having bad habits too! Remember that mirroring is a surgical tool: you only use it in small, specific ways. You don't substitute another person's judgment for your own. You just model the behavior you aspire to for reasons of your own.

Balance

Your brain wants all four of the happy chemicals. You are probably better at some than others, and it's tempting to choose a remodeling project in the area you're already good at. That may be good for your first circuit-building project, but after that, give your brain the happy chemical it is missing. You may have to enter unknown territory to do that, but the risk will bring great rewards. For example:

- If you are already a "dopamine kind of person," good at setting goals and meeting them, you could do more for yourself by working on a different happy chemical.
- If you are already an "oxytocin person," good at social bonding, you'd get higher returns by investing your effort in a different area.
- If you're a "serotonin person," good at winning respect, you can flourish by developing other happy-chemical circuits.
- If you tend to be an "endorphin person," drawn to mastering pain, you could benefit from focusing elsewhere.

When you depend on one happy chemical more than others, you don't know what's missing because you equate happiness with the kind you already have. So try a project from each of the four happy chemicals. It's not easy, but your brain will thank you.

DIFFERENT KINDS OF BALANCE

Balancing your neurochemistry is not the same as "work-life balance." It's true that spending too much time at work can lead to neglect of other needs. But if you leave work to run the same circuits in your free time, neurochemical balance will not happen. If you manage your home the way you manage your work, free time won't make you happier. It's like a vegetarian trying to balance with a new vegetable, or an athlete balancing with a new sport. You keep seeking rewards in familiar places until you discover new places.

The good news is that a little bit of the missing neurochemical goes a long way. You don't need to make huge changes to feel big results. Your brain rewards you for taking the neural road-not-taken. But it won't release the new happy chemical immediately. You have to invest the time it takes to build the infrastructure.

Graft

You can graft a new branch onto the roots of a happy circuit you've already developed. When old people reconnect with high-school sweethearts, they are grafting new circuits onto old roots. Returning to a hobby you loved as a child or building a hobby into a career are other well-known grafting successes. Adding branches to an existing tree is a good way to overcome the difficulty of building brand-new happy circuits.

When I retired from academia, I began judging science fairs. I love this new limb on my old trunk. I meet kids that I deeply respect, and they are thrilled to have professional attention given to their work. I've also learned to use my love of color to make difficult things fun. When I work on a slide presentation or my newsletter, I enjoy designing the colors. It may seem trivial, but a pinch of spice is all it takes to enhance a dish.

Grafting is also a good way to balance your neurochemicals. You can spark the happy chemical that's difficult for you by grafting onto an activity you love. If you love photography, for example, you are stimulating dopamine when you seek and find a particular shot. You can also stimulate oxytocin if you share the images with others, and serotonin by entering your pictures in exhibitions. If you're a person who loves parties, you are already stimulating oxytocin. You can stimulate dopamine by planning parties, and serotonin by organizing fundraisers. New happy-chemical pathways are easier to spark when you build on existing roots.

Energy

Your brain only has a limited amount of energy. You can enhance it with exercise, sleep, and good nutrition, but it will still be limited. New behaviors consume more energy than you expect. When you commit to a forty-five day rewiring project, you commit to making that energy available. If you run out of energy before meeting your daily commitment, you will find reasons to ditch it. So make your new habit the top-priority use of your energy for forty-five days, even if you have to relax another priority.

One way to ensure energy is to schedule your new habit first thing in the morning. If that's impossible, do something fun right before your challenging new behavior or right after. Watch a rerun of your favorite TV show in the middle of the day if that's what it takes. Activating new neurons takes more energy that you realize, and some planning is needed to make that energy available.

Mental energy is a lot like physical energy. It depends on glucose, and it takes time to restore once depleted. You easily succumb to temptations when your mental energy is depleted. Some experts advise eating sugar to boost your mental energy. This is obviously a flawed long-term strategy, even though it helps to bring a candy bar into a life-changing exam for a short-term boost. A glucose-spiking habit will literally hurt your survival, even though it creates the illusion of strength for a moment. You need other ways to sustain your mental energy for forty-five days.

Legacy

Anything connected to your DNA triggers happy chemicals. For most of human history, children came unplanned, and grandchildren came if you survived to your forties. Whatever enhanced their survival prospects made you happy. Things have changed, and alternative ways to feel your legacy are being explored. Some people research their ancestry, and others make an effort to preserve family traditions. You don't consciously connect this to your genes, but your happy chemicals turn on when you promote the survival of your unique individual essence. Even if you just buy pizza for a niece or nephew, it feeds your inner mammal's interest in the survival of your genes. You may say genes don't matter, but your brain has a curious way of perking up when they're involved.

There are infinite ways to satisfy your mammal brain's quest for a legacy. You might invent a stitch that lives on at your knitting club. You might design a new exercise machine at your gym club. A smoothie might be named after you at the corner store. It doesn't have to make logical sense. When something of you can live on, it's strangely effective at triggering happy chemicals.

Connecting with children rewards the urge for legacy even if they're not yours. If you do have children of your own, every moment with them is part of your legacy whether or not it's obvious. I figured this out when my son's school closed for teacher training. Parents complained about all the no-school days, and I admit I had the I-should-be-working feeling too. Then I learned to see it as a gift: Here was an extra chance to invest in my kids. I would be crazy to see it as a burden.

Fun

Repetition is easier to tolerate if you can make it fun. I've had fun learning foreign languages by traveling and watching movies, and people have learned languages "on the pillow" (*sur l'oreiller*, as they say in French) since before there were pillows.

One reason adults don't build new circuits is that they neglect the power of fun. Find the fun in a new behavior and you'll free yourself from the drawbacks of your old amusements. Sometimes we need to do things that aren't fun, of course. But finding the fun in an activity helps you persist long enough to pave the path.

Fun is a great energy-management tool. If I am working on something extra-hard, I take a fun break in the middle. I leave time for fun every evening so I can face challenges the next day. I never waste my fun time on movies about death and dismemberment. I don't waste it on hostile, angry pundits, even though others think they're funny. I don't waste it on restaurants with long lines, loud noise, and the prospect of going to bed on a full stomach. I am choosy about my fun because my energy is my most valuable resource.

Chunk

The brain is always dividing things into chunks because it can only process a few inputs at a time. Most of the time we don't notice this chunking strategy, but you can consciously divide your challenges into chunks to make them feel manageable. A cyclist I know reaches the top of a mountain by mentally dividing it into quarters. He focuses his attention on the next quarter-post and mentally celebrates when he reaches it. This makes no logical sense, because the mountain is just as high. But chunking can trick your brain into feeling good even when you're not really fooled.

When I learned this trick from the cyclist, I tried it on my own "mountain"—the mess in my garage. I was amazed at how well it worked. My husband and I both dreaded the chore, but longed to have it done. I suggested that we tackle it for fifteen minutes, and leave the rest for another day. I thought we would get it done in fifteen-minute chunks, but once we got started, we didn't feel like stopping. We could not climb our junk mountain when we stood at the bottom and looked up because the top was too high. But when we set our sights on an easy goal, we expected to succeed, and the good feeling triggered the next step, and the next. Positive expectations can spark a fire of enthusiasm.

Satisfice

Our brains are good at finding satisfactory solutions, fast. Sometimes we regret them later as we imagine the ideal thing we coulda-woulda-shoulda done. The urge to make the most of life is natural, but if you're always optimizing, you're never happy. When I find it hard to stop optimizing, I remind myself that the 1978 Nobel Prize in Economics was awarded to a mathematical proof that "satisficing" is better than optimizing. Herbert Simon showed us why embracing a satisfactory solution is better than investing in endless analysis.

I can always find a way that I fell short, even when I do well. When I see an adorable toddler, I fault myself for letting my children's toddlerhood slip away. Then I remind myself that optimizing is impossible, and I am good at satisficing.

So instead of passing up a good parking spot in hopes of finding a better one, I take the satisfactory spot and feel good about it. If I'm left with a long walk, I feel good about the fact that I am walking rather than driving around in circles. Feeling good about the satisfactory solution stops you from wasting energy on a protracted search whose marginal benefits will not exceed marginal costs.

Plan

Build a new circuit before you need it. Try new vegetables before you get bored with the old ones. Do someone a favor before you need a favor from her. Develop new sources of pride before you retire and get wrinkles. You may feel too busy to do these things now, but once they trigger happy chemicals, you'll be glad you did. Instead of waiting for happy chemicals to come your way, plan to "do something."

Planning is also a good way to relieve unhappy chemicals. Instead of worrying all day, plan to worry while brushing your teeth. If that's not enough, plan to worry while you floss too. In forty-five days, you will love the results.

Visualize

If you were prescribed two weeks of antibiotics to cure an infection, you would visualize the success of the treatment even though you couldn't see it. You wouldn't double your dose on Day Two if you weren't cured on Day One, nor would you stop the treatment on Day Three if you already felt better. You imagine your cells developing even without visible progress. It would be nice to have visible evidence of your new neural pathway, but you can stay the course by visualizing your developing brain cells.

Once your new pathway is established, your happy habit will feel so natural that you will literally forget to feel bad.

EXERCISE: HOW WILL YOU USE YOUR TOOLS?

I will use these tools to make my new happy habit more comfortable:

_____

_____

_____

_____

_____

_____

_____

_____

THESE TOOLS WILL HELP YOU TRAIN YOUR BRAIN

Mirror: find someone with the habit you want and mirror them.

Balance: develop the happy chemicals you're not already best at.

Graft: build new happy circuits onto old happy roots.

Energy: save your energy for tough challenges.

Legacy: preserve your unique individual essence to please your inner mammal.

Fun: find the fun in a new behavior and you will repeat it.

Chunk: divide difficult challenges into smaller parts.

Satisfice: a satisfactory solution may be better than an endless quest for optimal.

Plan: start building circuits now so they're ready when you need them.

Visualize: your neural pathways are building even though they're not visible.

Let In the Good

Our cortex is designed to learn from patterns, and we often look for the pattern in our mistakes. We can end up focused on what goes wrong and forget to notice what goes right.

Animals don't dwell on their errors. A mouse who fails to get the cheese tries again without kicking herself for being an idiot. She is not expecting to get the cheese on the first try every time. She is only trying to fill her belly.

A lizard approaches life with a very simple decision model: When he sees something bigger than himself, he runs. When he sees something smaller than himself, he tries to eat it. If he sees something about his size, he tries to mate with it. This decision tree leads to a lot of mistakes, so a lizard has a lot of ups and downs. But he doesn't expect to be up all the time. He doesn't judge himself for his downs or compare himself to other lizards.

A big brain is good at keeping score on itself. Learning from your mistakes has value, of course, but your error-analysis habit can crowd out your awareness of the good. You can focus on what goes wrong in the world so intently that you don't see what goes right.

I learned to notice what goes right after spending a year in Africa. Before that, I took flush toilets for granted, but I learned that people did without sewage systems for most of human history. When we have them, it doesn't make us happy, but open sewage ditches and vermin-infested outhouses might make you unhappy. I learned to appreciate the work of my municipal waste institution instead of just finding fault with it.

My appreciation of infrastructure began in Haiti, when I was invited to a picnic at a dam. "Why would you want to picnic at a dam," I asked. I had lived in the world where dams were sneered at as blots on the landscape. My coworker explained that electricity and drinking water were scarce, and the dam was widely seen as something to celebrate. Since then, every time I use water, I think about all it took to get it to me. When I wash a teacup, I imagine the quantity of water I've used in relation to the containers Haitian women carry on their heads. I value all that goes into these systems instead of just looking for their flaws.

During my stays in China, I went for many massages. I marveled at the fact that I could safely hand over my credit card and take my clothes off on the other side of the earth. That level of trust is a colossal achievement. In most of human history, it was not safe to leave your village. Strangers could kill you with impunity, so people rarely left their hamlets in a lifetime. Now, strangers literally rub shoulders worldwide in safety. Things go wrong occasionally, but when you focus on that, you miss the enormity of what goes right.

In my travels, I've seen a lot of food contaminated by insects, vermin, and grains of sand, not to mention invisible toxins. For most of human history, people welcomed contaminated food because it was better than hunger. Today's food supply has been purified to an extraordinary degree. Yet many people rage at the food industry and panic over food risks without perspective on what they have.

The same is true of healthcare. Our endless information about health risks makes it easy to focus on the faults of healthcare and overlook its accomplishments. I would not be alive today if it weren't for antibiotics, so I was surprised to learn that they did not even exist a decade before I was born. Most of us alive today would already have been done in by something without modern healthcare, yet people tend to rage at healthcare with scarcely a thought of what goes right.

Raging at the flaws of the world is a habit that's easy to build. Many people even see it as a skill to be proud of. They don't know they're in a vicious cycle that keeps them focused on disaster scenarios in order to keep feeling good about themselves. But we all have a choice.

Expectations and a Box of Chocolates

Choosing a chocolate from a box brings the risk of disappointment. To make matters worse, you may see someone else get the chocolate you'd hoped for. You can end up feeling bad even as you're enjoying intense chocolaty goodness. The difference between your dream chocolate and your disappointing chocolate is extremely small, but that's what you focus on.

Your brain builds expectations about what will make you happy and it sees the world through the lens of those expectations. You can skip over the rest of the story because your brain is so focused on what worked before.

We all see the world through a lens built in adolescence because that's when the brain is highly plastic. This lens is inevitably unrealistic. A young person imagines she will feel on top of the world when she is free of homework and bedtime. But once she faces the challenge of meeting her own needs, she doesn't feel like a master of the universe and she wonders what went wrong.

You may think something is wrong with the world, or with your boss, your partner, your culture, yourself. You never blame the brain circuits that compare reality to your youthful expectations, because those circuits function without your awareness.

I have a friend who always complains about the food she gets in a restaurant. She chose it herself, of course, but once it comes, it seems flawed to her. She looks longingly at other people's orders. I feel like I can't enjoy my meal when I'm with her, so I no longer eat with this person.

I often hear students complain about the difficulty of choosing courses. But I also hear them complain when they have no choice because a course is required. They don't value choice when they have it, but they lament losing it.

If you had lived in times past, you wouldn't have been free to choose your career, your beliefs, or even your sex partner. You would have been constrained by group expectations. You would imagine eternal bliss if only you could choose your mate, your work, and other aspects of your life. Yet when you have these choices, they don't make you happy. Your brain keeps looking for more and focusing on the obstacles. It's just doing the job it was designed for.

Unhappiness is often blamed on "bad choices." This implies that "good choices" are available. The truth is more complicated. Each choice has advantages and disadvantages. Once you pick, you get to see the disadvantages of that choice up close. It's easy to imagine that all would be lovely if only the other choice were yours. But if a do-over were possible, chances are you'd be frustrated by another "bad choice." You could spend your whole life lamenting your choices if you don't make a habit of seeing the good in what you've chosen. And even a "good choice" can only make you happy for a short time, because happy chemicals only come in short spurts. So as we struggle to make "good choices," the first choice we must make is to manage our own happy chemicals.

If you decide to be happy, your brain will find things to be happy about. You will still have frustrations and disappointments, but you will find ways to make yourself happy anyway. If your happy pathways don't spark themselves, you will find healthy ways to crank them up.

You can do this right now.

No one is stopping you.

No one can do it for you.

And you cannot do it for someone else.

Your happy chemicals will not surge all the time, but you do not need to be having a "peak" experience at every moment. You can accept the inevitable dips in your happy chemicals instead of believing something is wrong. You don't have to mask the dips with unhealthy habits. You can just take them as evidence that your inner mammal is looking out for you in the best way it knows how.

It's not easy to manage this brain we've inherited from our ancestors. It's the challenge that comes with the gift of life.

KEEP IN TOUCH

Please sign up for my newsletter, *Private Lives of Primates*, at *www.InnerMammalInstitute.org*.

And write to me if you discover something amazing about the inner mammal. I'm especially interested in how you explain it to your friends, family, and coworkers.

Loretta@InnerMammalInstitute.org

RECOMMENDED READING

Here are some highly readable resources about the mammal brain. I winnowed down to the most engaging writing, and gave each book a unique Best in Category award to highlight my reasons for including it.

Best Place to Start

Life (the video documentary series)
Sir David Attenborough (creator), Oprah Winfrey (narrator)

This BBC series offers mesmerizing images of the behaviors that promote survival in nature. Attenborough explains the behaviors with his usual frankness and clarity, and Oprah Winfrey narrates the U.S. (Discovery Channel) edition. The images are stunning in their beauty and detail, and the story of how the images were captured makes it all the more riveting. I was so excited by this series that I tracked down every Attenborough series, and thus enjoyed an up-close and personal look at the survival behavior of mammals, reptiles, birds, insects, and even plants. Finally I realized that Attenborough is not the talking head; he's the driver of the technology that made it possible to capture images of wild behavior since the 1950s. His autobiography, *Life on Air*, is a very modest recounting of the perseverance that brought the facts of life to our living rooms. A knighthood richly deserved!

Best Can't-Put-It-Down Reading

A Primate's Memoir: A Neuroscientist's Unconventional Life among the Baboons
Robert Sapolsky

Sapolsky is a Stanford University School of Medicine professor who darts baboons in Africa to sample their neurochemicals. Sapolsky's careful linking of behavioral observation and neurochemical data has won scientific respect, but here he tells the personal story behind his work. He paints a vivid picture of the Masai villages and gun-toting game wardens that populated his workday on the Kenyan savannah. And he draws intriguing parallels between the social dynamics of academic science and the social dynamics of baboons.

Sapolsky's investigation of the sex hormones is reported in his *Monkeyluv* and *The Trouble with Testosterone*. But his chief contributions focus on the unhappy chemicals, better known as stress. Sapolsky searched for a link between stress and disease, and his popular *Why Zebras Don't Get Ulcers* reports those findings. As a fellow native of Brooklyn, I understand his interest in stress. But I also wanted to understand the happy chemicals, so I kept reading.

Best Description of How We Blend Conscious and Automatic Thought

How We Decide
Jonah Lehrer

This book shows how we combine our verbal and nonverbal thought processes when we make a decision. Lehrer marshals the latest research to explain why the best decisions rely heavily on the nonverbal processes. Individuals skilled at getting their conscious and unconscious minds to inform each other make better decisions. The author clarifies this skill with examples from daily life, from his difficulty choosing a breakfast cereal to a pilot's decisions during a crash landing. (Don't read on a plane!) Another brilliant book by the same author, *Proust Was a Neuroscientist*, shows how artists' descriptions of sensory experience correctly anticipated what science later learned about how we decode sensory inputs.

Best Introduction to the Social Anxiety of Primates

Chimpanzee Politics: Power and Sex Among Apes
Frans de Waal

If you find it hard to imagine how chimpanzees can plot and scheme for status, this book is for you. De Waal spent two years observing a large colony of captive chimps and wrote about their daily lives in soap-operatic detail. He describes the dangerous liaisons, the coalition building, and the constant social calculations that chimps engage in to get ahead in their world. His tales of chimp society will remind you of people you know, and you will come to appreciate how a brain can build complex social relationships without words. The twenty-fifth anniversary edition has good photos, too.

Best Explanation of the Emotional Roller Coaster

I, Mammal: Why Your Brain Links Status and Happiness
Loretta Graziano Breuning

Most people say they don't care about status, but small advances or setbacks in your social status trigger surprisingly strong emotions. This book explains why. It shows how the mammal brain rewards you with the good feeling of serotonin when you gain any small advantage over a rival. When you lose a small advantage, your mammal brain alarms you with the bad feeling of cortisol. It's not easy being a mammal, but the good-humored depiction of animal status-seeking is followed by a set of exercises for making peace with your inner status-seeker.

Best Description of Monkey Business

Macachiavellian Intelligence: How Rhesus Macaques and Humans Have Conquered the World
Dario Maestripieri

Monkeys are Macachiavellian, according to this Italian neurobiologist from the lab in Parma that discovered mirror neurons. Rhesus macaque monkeys are second only to humans in intelligence—if you define intelligence as the ability to survive in new environments. Macaques can survive anywhere, just like humans. They thrive all over the earth, even in the inner cities of Asia and the abandoned temples of tropical rain forests.

Their social skills are key to their ability to adapt to different environments. That doesn't mean they hold hands and sing "Kumbaya." This book describes macaques' social skills without a lot of sugar-coating or academic theory. We see how they pick their friends and lovers. We learn when they nurture their children and when they leave their children to develop independence. The empirical science is combined with lively stories of the private lives of monkeys observed in the wild. I loved it!

Best Challenge to the Disease-Based View of the Brain

Anatomy of an Epidemic: Magic Bullets, Psychiatric Drugs, and the Astonishing Rise of Mental Illness in America
Robert Whitaker

The limits of psychopharmacology are often debated with high emotion, but this book is not a simplistic rant at pill-pushers. It's a well-reasoned and highly readable exploration of the temptation to put one's faith in behavioral medicine. The limits and tradeoffs of meds are clearly delineated, and the promise of alternatives is explored.

Best Introduction to the Human Brain

How the Mind Works
Steven Pinker

Pinker explains the findings of neuroscience in everyday language with clever references to popular culture. He goes where the evidence leads instead of jumping on intellectual bandwagons. Our physiological endowment makes us much more than just the product of cultural training, he asserts. More on the evolutionary foundations of human thought can be found in his excellent book *The Blank Slate: The Modern Denial of Human Nature*.

Best Field Research

Baboon Metaphysics: The Evolution of a Social Mind
Dorothy L. Cheney and Robert M. Seyfarth

When Charles Darwin was in his twenties, he wrote in his notebook: "He who understands the baboon would do more toward metaphysics than Locke." Cheney and Seyfarth take up Darwin's challenge by conducting simple experiments on wild baboons. For example, they record baboons' diverse vocalizations and play them back to analyze the responses of other baboons. Their findings illuminate links between social behaviors and reproductive success. Baboons constantly make sophisticated social judgments about mating and child nurturing. Being a social creature does not mean being "nice" to everyone all the time, and this book shows how a baboon decides whom to favor and when. The authors' earlier work on vervet monkeys, *How Monkeys See the World*, also sheds great light on how the primate brain goes about meeting its survival needs.

Best Antidote to Negativity

Beyond Cynical: Transcend Your Mammalian Negativity
Loretta Graziano Breuning

Cynicism is popular because it feels good. It helps you feel superior to others (serotonin), to build social bonds (oxytocin), and to redefine rewards so they feel approachable (dopamine). But you have to stay focused on the negative to enjoy the good feeling of cynicism. This book offers a way out of that vicious cycle, and it sustains the momentum of the present volume. You can rewire yourself to feel good in the world you actually live in instead of letting your happiness wait for the promised land of your imagination.

Best Introduction to the Human Limbic System

The Emotional Brain: The Mysterious Underpinnings of Who We Are
Joseph LeDoux

This is a clear description of the brain systems we've inherited from earlier mammals, especially the amygdala. It helps us make the link between our body parts and our subjective perceptions, and thus to notice the mental activity we conduct with neurochemicals rather than with words. The book tilts toward the negative emotions such as fear, and on disease rather than normalcy. But it is still a highly accessible description of what goes on under the hood. LeDoux's other great work, *Synaptic Self: How Our Brains Become Who We Are*, is a great explanation of how we store old experiences and retrieve them to process new experiences.

Best Compilation of Happiness Research

The Science of Happiness: How Our Brains Make Us Happy—and What We Can Do to Get Happier
Stefan Klein

Klein introduces the broad array of research on happiness in a highly accessible style. The book has no overarching theory, but it is a good way to extend one's knowledge of the happy chemicals.

Best Conceptualization of Nonverbal Thought

Animals in Translation
Temple Grandin

The author is a person with autism who works as a consultant in livestock management. She believes her autism helps her understand how animals think. She explains that animals see more detail than humans. Humans learn to ignore details once we find the abstract pattern in those details. Grandin is good at avoiding the idealized notions about animals that result from projecting one's ideal world onto the animal world. Her insights are based on a lifetime of direct experience with farm animals, as well as a PhD in animal science. Her descriptions of animal thinking help us understand our own brain's reactions to the world beneath the verbal abstractions that dominate our attention.

Best Insight into a Happy Home and a Happy Club

The Territorial Imperative: A Personal Inquiry Into the Animal Origins of Property and Nations
Robert Ardrey

The most monogamous primate is the gibbon, so one naturally wonders how they keep the magic alive. It seems that couples team up to fight the neighbors, thus defending the fruit trees that keep their children alive. This book is a fascinating description of animals' wide-ranging social dominance behaviors. The patterns are eerily familiar, and Ardrey clearly shows how they're produced by natural selection rather than conscious intent. People's strong attachment to their own little corner of the world makes sense once you read this book.

Best Introduction to Our Neurochemistry

Molecules of Emotion: The Science Behind Mind-Body Medicine
Candace Pert

This science memoir is a perfect blend of neuroscience and the personal story of the researcher. Candace Pert was an early advocate of the idea that chemicals cause emotion. She was central to the discovery of opiate receptors in the brain, which led to the understanding that the body makes its own opiates.

Best Insight into Mammalian Social Dominance

Cesar's Way: The Natural, Everyday Guide to Understanding and Correcting Common Dog Problems
Cesar Millan

This is not just a "dog" book. It explains the workings of the mammal brain using dog experiences familiar to everyone. We have all seen dogs struggling for dominance. Millan realized that dogs get agitated when the status hierarchy is unclear. They keep trying to assert dominance until they are dominated. They are calmer when hierarchical relations are established. This book tells the fascinating tale of how Millan figured this out. He grew up on a Mexican farm with working dogs. He saw that they weren't aggressive like his neighbors' dogs because his grandfather led them. He never met a "pet" until he moved to Hollywood. There, he met extremely neurotic pets that are loved and coddled but can't stop struggling for dominance. His life experience makes a great story and a great contribution to our understanding of the mammal brain.

Best Child Development Book

NurtureShock: New Thinking about Children
Po Bronson and Ashley Merryman

Bronson had children later in life and expected them to mold into his well-meaning hands. He discovered that kids learn from what you do rather than what you say. Who knew? This inspired him to study neuroscience and revisit his long-held presumptions about how "our society" should manage "our children." He explores the way a child's mind learns from direct interpersonal experience, not from preachy theories about how the world should work. It makes perfect sense when you understand mirror neurons (which are not directly addressed in the book).

Bronson confronts his own illusion that constant praise can help a kid get ahead. Effusive praise for mediocre effort gives the wrong message, he realizes. Kids are good observers of what gets rewarded and what doesn't. If mediocre effort gets big praise, kids don't build trust in their own abilities. Bronson struggled to restrain his urge to shower his children with accolades. His honesty about that makes the book humorous and engaging. Unfortunately, Bronson doesn't acknowledge his own preoccupation with his children's future status. Readers familiar with mammalian social dominance will see it clearly.

Best Social History of Our Natural Status Urge

Status Anxiety
Alain de Botton

This book explores the reasons why status bugs us and what we can do about it. The human preoccupation with the good opinion of others has been dissected by philosophers for millennia. Alain de Botton is a British philosopher with an entertaining style and a refreshing lack of bitterness. He provides a riveting history of bohemians, whose conspicuous rejection of bourgeois values often masked a private life consumed by the pursuit of money, fame, and one-upmanship. He explores the temptation to blame the world for the common feeling that we have fallen short in some way. The book brims with historical examples, such as duels over "honor," and shows how status anxiety has always been a part of human life.

De Botton has written many other books on happiness that are philosophical without being deadly dull. His writing will especially appeal to readers with a more literary and historical than scientific bent.

Best Classic

Sociobiology
Edward O. Wilson

This is the book that started it all, and it's good reading despite being born as a textbook. It walks you through the social behavior of a huge array of animals, making the survival value of each behavior absolutely clear. You will see a lot of patterns that remind you of people you know.

Best Oldie

The Dragons of Eden: Speculations on the Evolution of Human Intelligence
Carl Sagan

This book won a 1978 Pulitzer Prize, and it's easy to see why. Sagan's famous skill for speculation and popularization are applied here to the distant past rather than distant galaxies. The title refers to the reptilian fears that the first humans might have inherited. Fortunately, the book speculates on the pleasant as well as the unpleasant emotions of our earliest ancestors. Sagan's ideas about human cognition have been largely validated by the neuroscience that came decades later. And he dares to be positive, saying, "If this is where we have come from, we have come very far."

Best Picture Book on Human Progress

The Good Old Days: They Were Terrible!
Otto L. Bettmann

Historical cartoon drawings are used to illustrate the unpleasant aspects of days gone by. The author is an eminent historian and founder of the picture archive at the New York Public Library. He brings humor to his descriptions of the insecurity and harshness of daily life in the past. The book conquers the widely held presumption that life has gotten worse in modern times.

Best Explanation of "Hard-Wiring"

The Talent Code: Greatness Isn't Born, It's Grown
Daniel Coyle

The author sets out to explain why so many top performers in a field often come from one training center. Coyle investigates these "hotbeds of talent" to learn what these trainers are doing right. The answer he finds rests on a little-known aspect of brain function: the myelination of neurons. Repetition builds the myelin sheaths that make neurons efficient. Great talent develops when we repeat difficult skills enough to myelinate bundles of neurons. We all have plenty of myelinated neural pathways as a result of repeated early experience. But we often get frustrated when we strive to build such pathways consciously. Coyle's research uncovered the distinctive kind of repetition that best promotes myelination and thus new skills.

Best Hope for the Future

An Unchanged Mind: The Problem of Immaturity in Adolescence
by John McKinnon

Maturity doesn't just come automatically with time. It has to be learned. We're all born helpless and need others to meet our needs. We are soothed by the expectation that others will meet our needs, and learn to survive by calling attention to our needs. Yet we all must gradually learn to meet our own needs. What if this shift doesn't happen? What if a person expects others to meet his or her needs forever? They may not expect this consciously, but the reward structure in their life may have trained it into them. The resulting immature behavior gets labeled as a "disease" in the modern world. It's not a disease—it's a learning gap that can be solved by learning. If you didn't learn realistic expectations and self-care skills in the past, you can learn them now. McKinnon has written a sequel to help: *To Change a Mind: Parenting to Promote Maturity in Teenagers.*

INDEX

ABOUT THE AUTHOR

Loretta Graziano Breuning grew up surrounded by unhappiness and was determined to make sense of it. She was not convinced by theories of human motivation she learned in school, so she kept searching. When she learned about the effect brain chemicals have on animals, human frustrations suddenly made sense, so she retired from teaching and founded the Inner Mammal Institute.

Dr. Breuning holds a PhD from Tufts and a BS from Cornell, both in multidisciplinary social science. She is Professor Emerita of Management at California State University, East Bay. Her other books include *I, Mammal: Why Your Brain Links Status and Happiness* and *The Science of Positivity*. She writes the blog *Your Neurochemical Self* on PsychologyToday.com.

The Inner Mammal Institute provides tools that help people make peace with the animal inside. It has helped thousands of people learn to manage their neurochemical ups and downs. Discover your inner mammal at *www.InnerMammalInstitute.org*.

After college, Ms. Breuning spent a year in Africa as a United Nations Volunteer. She experienced the corruption that undermines economic development and resolved to teach her students an alternative. She wrote the book *Grease-le$$: How to Thrive*

Without Bribes in Developing Countries, and has lectured on that subject in China, Armenia, the Philippines, and Albania.

Today, she volunteers as a docent at the Oakland Zoo, where she gives tours on mammalian social behavior. And she marvels each day at the overlap between a wildlife documentary and the lyrics to popular love songs.